Theology of Work and Development

The Theological and Ecological

Responsibility of the Church

in Sustainable Development

Theology of Work and Development

The Theological and Ecological

Responsibility of the Church

in Sustainable Development

Elly Kansiime

Globethics.net Praxis No. 15

Globethics.net Praxis

Director: Prof. Dr. Obiora Ike, Executive Director of Globethics.net in Geneva and Professor of Ethics at the Godfrey Okoye University Enugu/Nigeria.

Globethics.net Praxis Series 15
Elly Kansiime, *Theology of Work and Development: The Theological and Ecological Responsibility of the Church in Sustainable Development*
Geneva: Globethics.net, 2020
ISBN 978-2-88931-373-0 (online version)
ISBN 978-2-88931-374-7 (print version)
© 2020 Globethics.net

Managing Editor: Ignace Haaz
Layout and cover design: Michael Cagnoni

Globethics.net International Secretariat
150 route de Ferney
1211 Geneva 2, Switzerland
Website: *www.globethics.net/publications*
Email: *publications@globethics.net*

All web links in this text have been verified as of October 2020.

TABLE OF CONTENTS

FOREWORD

This piece of work on the role of the church in sustainable development, intends to bring out the theological and ecological responsibility the church observes as she engages in development, but equally important as she engages with the people. The church is a major player because of the big numbers that constitute her institution. She has an everyday opportunity, and over binding responsibility to fulfill her ministry mandate. The church is one of the front line players in development, and her place is vital because she is supposed to engage a holistic role in development, more than any other player does. The church is relational in the sense that she represents a relational God. The writer looks at development from a divine perspective, and expects all developers, to integrate the biblical teaching in development so that it can make meaning and sustain God's creation.

The writer looks at how development has degraded the environment in the names of urbanization, industrialization, and globalization. All these dimensions have been pointed out as being responsible for destroying the environment in the name of development. The outcome has shown that the environment that would have sustained life has instead become less efficient in providing conducive life. The future generations appear to be facing threats of being displaced and later wiped out, because what remains, cannot hold life for long.

A set of picture have been gathered to show the extent of environmental degradation, especially basing on the building and construction industries. The key players are individuals for small-scale projects, and companies for large-scale projects. The marks left behind have been unintentional, but negative to life. Besides, the write has ventured into other areas of human behavior that are non-compliant to sustainable development. To a greater extent, the church has been held responsible, because of her silence and at the same time her failure to realize the importance of theological and ecological tools.

The church locally and globally has been sighted as having a large membership in position to influence sustainable development, and a good number of them are in positions of leadership at all levels. However, it has been noted that, human as they are, they are prone to vices that influence unsustainable development. Such vices include pride, greed, envy, lust and laziness. They deny people from understanding their individual mandate and contributions to sustainable development. They are who they are despite their unified purpose in development.

To all of those who will have an opportunity to read this book, regardless of your faith or traditional beliefs, it will broaden your personal scope of engagement in sustainable development. It will also help you, the reader, to understand that we are a generation preparing for the generations to come, as the past generations did for us. As this generation passes on, a new one will come to build on what we shall leave behind for them. Therefore, the writer argues us to be very cautious as we engage in development, no matter the level or degree. You are persuaded to read this book and see where you are placed as an individual, and how you can influence sustainable development.

PREFACE

Development, though well-defined and having many people engage in it, it has always taken a little bit of shallow understanding, where by some other areas of human life have been neglected or overlooked. Wherever there has been development, there has always been environmental problems. Many times, governments, companies and individuals, have seen development from one particular angle; the economic benefit. Studies might be made to portray a picture that developmental projects are beneficial to the citizens, while inwardly the central focus is on how much money the project would bring to the government or individual project owners. Whereas it is true that environmental impact assessment is always done, developers have been known to conceal the long-term negative impact. Some of the examples that have been given, are like copper mining in Kasese fifty years ago, which has left a very big negative impact on the eco-system. Many mega industries and projects have displaced people and animals, destroyed water catchment areas, cleared off big chunks of forest cover, and degraded riverbanks and lakeshores. Since individuals with a lot of money own big companies, they have the money and power to protect their projects, and therefore no one can stop them.

The position of the church in such development is very important; because she has the divine voice to guide, the direction development should take, if God's creation is to be sustained. Not all developers are necessarily Bible readers, and therefore they might not understand what the Bible says about development. The church's role is to teach her members on how to use their environment for sustainable development, and become agents of change. However, the church must be conversant with her theological and ecological responsibilities while carrying out any kind of development.

concepts act like an acid test or blue litmus paper test in a laboratory. With the spiritual concepts, developers can be helped to move easily towards sustainable development.

Therefore, the writer intends to draw our attention to the thinking that can help all development players to begin moving towards engaging sustainable development that is holistic in nature, by encouraging the church to participate from a theological and ecological perspective. The church is a divine institution with a divine calling in God's creation. She has a role to play. Apart from the using development to supporting life in many different ways, the writer is of the view that developers need to be creative. The book therefore, looks at the way the heart, head and hands work together if sustainable development has to be realized. The moment the three are separated, especially the heart from the head and hands, there will be misguided and degraded development. Because of human efforts and failures, development has been focusing on individual benefits, and has resulted into many faults, affecting the environment negatively. For that matter, the church stands to be blamed for failing to put things in order because she knows the truth about what must be done from the Biblical mandate given at creation; to rule and work by replenishing the earth.

However, having seen development disregarding this mandate, the argument then is that the environment must be redeemed since Jesus Christ has redeemed humanity. Human beings cannot be redeemed outside what they do. A redeemed humanity redeems the lost work values. That is why our God remains rational and relational through his work. He cannot late it crumple down, when the church as his voice has been placed here on earth to bring complete redemption, thus the consummation of the redeemed creation. Developers are encouraged to see rationale in their work, because it must not be done for the pleasure of humanity, but instead, for relating with God the creator. They must see development as one of the areas of stewardship, and they are therefore mandated to do it as God's managers. That is why, it is important that wherever development of any kind is done, people must experience the joy it brings, instead of painful experiences.

As a matter of importance, development which is part of what we do, has to be seen as a sacred engagement and not secular. That is when it will realize sustainable goals or results. The book reminds us that we shall all give accountability of what we do as part of development. This call for individual responsibility whenever we are working, no matter the magnitude of our work or development projects. It has been pointed out that, our development engagements have cosmic scope. What we do here, eventually affects people elsewhere. The environmental degradation for example, has had negative climatic changes all over the world. We share the vast eco system, and therefore one part of the world influences the other in many different ways. Therefore, when we engage development reasonably and innovatively, it will be one of the indicators that the fallen work has been restored.

Besides the environmental problems pointed out already, there are also other forces surrounding human life, which are not sustainable in development. One of such forces the book brings out is foreign economic dependence. This has greatly affected the developing countries in their endeavor to build their physical infrastructures, stable economic base, and social structures. When there is an economic crunch as it were in the early 2000's, most of the beneficiaries of the foreign funding crumbled down almost in everything. This was an indicator that foreign dependence was not sustainable to development.

As much has been said about the role of the church in sustainable development, nevertheless, there are challenges and problems that have been pointed out facing the church's participation in mitigating sustainable development. These included political influences, economic positioning, theological interpretation, and traditional beliefs. There are also moral hindrances to sustainable development, which can be dealt with spiritually.

I

INTRODUCTION

1. Introduction

Sustainability is what has kept human life on going for generations. It does not matter in which area of life one is engaged, we all work for our livelihood, and this livelihood is interpersonal, surpassing individual needs. The Church's role in development is a fundamental matter if life has to be lived joyfully and meaningfully. God put in place mechanisms that would sustain our life here on earth. However, the responsibility was entrusted to human beings, to work as God's stewards in his estate.

However, development to most people has usually been used as a 'blanket' terminology to mean a process of physical or structural growth, which may seem to overlook other human developments within their environment. The common global understanding of development always focuses on infrastructure, and population growth (people and animals), and economy in terms of inputs and outputs. However, the development of any nation can be expanded to include all other characteristics of social, religious, political, and economic concerns that if holistically considered, will determine sustainable development. Whereas other areas might be factors contributing to sustainable development, the most vital and central, but much neglected area is the spiritual aspect, which gives us a Theology of Work. It is the positive driving force behind every sensible and profitable development. Infrastructures will be put in place, people will get employment and income of considerable degree will be realized, population will increase, but if what they do and earn do not involve a theology of work, it will not be sustainable.

When we fail to demystify or indicate development holistically, we may lead to the neglect of very important aspects of sustainable development. Yet, it is very clear that at no point in time, can a nation realize complete development in all aspects of human life, without considering the social, political, economic and spiritual dimensions together, since all of them interact towards sustainable development. Therefore development should is measured from a holistic, but mainly from a spiritual and religious perspective, given that different levels of attainment can be evaluated using the spiritual or religious barometer, of which the church is the agent.

Whereas development seem to be a struggle of attaining economic status, the political status of a nation has a great influence, in that the quality of governance must be very clear in its developmental goals. Political governance is one of the institutions put in place to enforce civil laws and order among the citizens to realize stable development, but sometimes it can cause instability in the process of putting up developmental projects and programs, which might not be oriented and addressed to human essential needs. While the political leaders plan to develop the people and their nations, they must put in consideration other players like the religious and social institutions, which have a great exposure to a large population of people at any given single moment. In that case, religious institutions like the church would be very much at the center of playing a primary role in sustainable development whether locally or globally. However, the church must have the moral credibility to engage developers, because it has been found out that the church has little expertise in dealing with developmental issues. As a spiritual organ within a nation, and one of the key players, she must train her leaders to become agents of sustainable development as of primary importance, to ensure that there is a holistic balance towards sustainable development, springing from individuals to communities.

In this book, we shall be looking at how the church participates in sustainable development, her theological and ecological responses to development, and what she must do in order to guard her ministry mandate entrusted to her. Therefore, we may ask ourselves, what it mean for the Church to be involved in development. The church herself from a theological point of view, is an institution of belonging as Bromiley says that the Church is belonging to the Lord, an understanding derived from the Greek word *kuriakos...(or)... ekklesia* denoting an assembly; an equivalent for the congregation of the Old Testament.[1] In other words, that which belongs to God. Another simple definition tells us that a "...Church is that collection of human societies which is inspired by, and seeks to characterize, the significance of Jesus".[2] Heinle calls it "the whole of a Christian institution including all its churches, members, and beliefs"[3]. Being identified as 'belonging to God' puts her in a position to understand her role in the world where she is placed among God's people. This then justifies our convictions of what the church can do or not do as her members get to think and be involved in 'development' that can sustain God's creation. It should doubtlessly be said that the church is the voice and work of God. She is a messenger and speaks from, about, and for God. In addition, she works with and through God. This simply tells us that when we become Christians, we constitute a society or community bonded by common beliefs. We become believers and servants of the one we follow. We speak and work according to what God has put in us. What Jesus Christ would have done personally is

---

[1] Geoffrey W. Bromiley, in his article "Church" in the *Bible Dictionary* edited by J. D. Douglas (Grand Rapids, Michigan: Zondervan, 1987), pp.218-9.

[2] N.J. Biggar in his article, "Church", in the *New Dictionary of Ethics & Pastoral Studies* by J. Atkinson et al. (England: IVP, 1995), p.229.

[3] Philip M. Rideout, *Newbury House Dictionary of American English (4th edn.)*, (USA: Monroe Allen Publishers, 2004), p.140.

done through us, his church. Jesus Christ demonstrated how human capacities could discern and practice what was and is right through both his human and divine work; and this explains how far the church's work in development can stretch. The church is made up of people from all lifestyles, sharing their wealth of talents to be put together for God's work. The church is not only limited to spiritual work but also in what God can allow her to inscribe on the face of the earth through the hands of her members in order to portray his presence. In this case, it would not be wrong to say that God has put his mind in the church institution to be passed on to others for the benefits of God's creation. The church's work is not a phenomenon of human will but one of God's higher calling for humanity. It matters a lot for those called and equipped to do specialized work in the church, for them, God has additionally skilled them or given them different gifts from what others in 'general' can do. The "general" here is used to include even those who are outside the community of Jesus followers, but have also been found to share in the work of the creator, although they may not be of the same beliefs as the Church members do. Warren says that; "Your call to salvation included your call to service."[4] The church is an institution of service saved from both spiritual and physical adversaries, and issues affecting sustainable development, where she must be visible from what she does different from the rest of the other institutions.

Therefore, this then makes us say that those who constitute the church have been better equipped for working much better than others, because they have got special calling, additional skilling and gifting, and can become good examples. For that matter, we can relevantly address ourselves to the primary role of the Church in the Local and Global Sustainable Development, which is really nothing less than working like the one who called the church and instructed her to genuine work en-

---

[4] Rick Warren, *The Purpose Driven Life* (Grand Rapids, Michigan: Zondervan, 2002), p.229.

gagements. The Church does share a lot in life with other faiths, before she can prove her working abilities to be worth of her faith in maintaining a sustainable development, from a local setting before she can influence the global concerns. Development, the world over, makes sense when it is liberated from the influence of satanic powers like corruption, greed, jealousy, pride, laziness, malice and many others, which suffocate good developmental plans. We may not need to ask if Christians do engage in the same vices, because if they did not, the church would have had a convincing voice to influence sustainable development. However, much as they may do, they have an advantage of being called to order by the one they have accepted to follow and serve, and then mend their ways, unlike others who are developers without the heart of Christ. A Christian bares the true image of Christ. However, that does not rule out that Christians cannot be manipulated, only the good thing with them is that Jesus teaching calls them to order. The Christian doctrine is so focused that it discourages corruption or manipulation of any kind of human life whether it deals with direct or indirect development. The church therefore becomes the vessel of order in working for sustainable development. She can influence the planning and the implementation of development if she plays her role very strategically and carefully. Sometimes it may not matter what ones faith or culture is or belongs to, because we know there is no community that shuts itself from the influence of others socially, economically, politically and religiously. There are many opportunities of synergy. In case some of us are not Christians, especially when we read from this book and find out the truth about what is said, we can improve on our developmental plans. It will not cost us anything to change our mindset and even our beliefs, and put them to work the way the Bible proposes.

2. Our Environment and Its Usage

Today there is a big outcry the world over due to the volatility of life as a result of misuse and risky usage of our environment and its natural resources in the name of development, which has resulted into unreliable global climatic conditions and untold healthy problems. We are not deaf to hear what is happening all over the world because of the climate changes threatening the existence of life on earth, and not blind to see what is happening around us. There are few local examples referred to here which can help us understand what negative impact development can do by threatening the existence and continuation of life when nations are carrying out mega infrastructural projects, which also later translate into major global environmental problems affecting life. In addition, there are those small developments made by individuals, scattered all over, which eventually tantamount to serious environmental problems. It is very important to note that development is key to the future of nations, but with very cautious planning of what the future will be, based on today's developmental goals.

3. Pictographic Evidence to Wetland Degradation in Uganda

In the pictures below, we are seeing a road infrastructure going through a forest. A number of things both negative and positive are happening. First of all depending on how far the road stretches through the forest, a large acreage of forest cover must be cut down to pave way for the road. Secondly, some soil must be sought for leveling the ground, and that means some other piece of land must be degraded for the sake of grading the new road. Thirdly, the ground level in some cases will be destabilized resulting into flooding and erosion. If there are so many road constructions of the kind, for sure they will affect the echo system and the climate there of. The pictures below were taken from Uganda roads infrastructural development projects. In other situations some soil for leveling was ferried from somewhere to make the project completed. This alone tells us that a number of animals and plant life was affected including the soils. We cannot run away from the truth that a development need translates into a life deficit of some degree that might never be reversed at all.

Picture 1: the forest road

Although building road infra-structure is good for sustaining transport, trade and increases national and international economic base, it threaten the importance of land forms and vital vegetation for the conducive climate, and agricultural productivity. It is said that such projects fragment and alter the habitat because when a road runs through a forest, it creates an edge habitat along the portion of the forest that fringes the road. Through altering the habitat and creating an edge, roads can affect animals even when direct mortality is not a result.

Picture 2 related to the mining industry.

The mining industry has destroyed very valuable cultivatable (agricultural) land and water sources because of the mineral processing industries like that of Kilembe mines- Kasese district in Uganda. Today as we speak, Kasese grapples with copper pollution. It is more than 36 years since the mining of copper at Kilembe Mines in Kasese district ended, but the effects are as fresh as if the industry is operative. A recently released research shows that high levels of metal concentrates including copper, cobalt, nickel, zinc and arsenic remain present in agricultural soils and public water sources[5].

4. Environmental Impact

Mining impact can occur at local, regional, and global levels through direct and indirect mining practices. Impact can result in erosion, sinkholes, loss of biodiversity, or the contamination of soil, groundwater, and surface water by the chemicals emitted from mining processes. These processes also have an impact on the atmosphere from the emissions of carbon, which have effect on the quality of human health and biodiversity.[6] Some mining methods may have such significant environmental and public health effects that mining companies in some countries are required to follow strict environmental and rehabilitation codes to ensure that the mined area returns to its original state. However, there is a lot of human innovation that can make development very friendly with and to the environment around us. The road construction below shows how developmental glitches could be avoided.

Picture 3: The Kampala, Entebbe road constructed between 2012 and 2018

---

[5] https://observer.ug/news/headlines/57987-kasese-grapples-with-copper-pollution.html Jun 20, 2018

[6] Laura J., Souter. *"Mining and Biodiversity: Key Issues and Research Needs in Conservation Science"* (Australia: The Royal Society Publishing, 2018), vol. 285, issue 1892.

The picture shows one of the ways in which destructive infrastructural development can be avoided when engaging mega projects. Instead of filling the swamp with marram or soil from some other place, the road was constructed in such a way that it did not interfere with the echo system.

5. The Position of the Church

In this perspective, it is worth bringing to our attention especially for the Church, to understand that she has a responsibility to be part of the national developmental programs, share views and even come up with alternative plans to save the environment and change the direction the world is moving in the name of development. The recently constructed Entebbe express high way in Uganda, has shown that we can avoid environmental degradation (see previous picture) by using other more friendly architectural designs that mega projects could still be put in place. In all there is need to evaluate the present against the future gains and the worth of the profits in relation to the worth of the people living today and thereafter. One may ask as to how the church can be involved in matters of national or international development interests. First, a number of countries that are at the apex of sustainable development, especially in the west, were and are still Christian countries guided by Christian values and principles. In Parliaments and Councils, international organizations and policy-making bodies, there are Christians of great influence who are well educated and good motion movers. The church above all has undisputed mandate to address people 24/7/12 without denial of addressing issues affecting the well-being of the people, because she is not only a voice but the holistic and divine voice of God. She has a Pulpit, the authorized and undisputed place where she proclaims the all- time word of God for the good of the people and the rest of creation. Besides the Pulpit, she has been mandated to preach in season and out of season (1Timothy…). What does she preach if she does not address local and global concerns affecting God's creation? When God pointed out in Hosea that his people were perishing because of ignorance, he went ahead and pointed out that the fault lay in the leaders -religious leaders, prophets and kings (Hosea.4:6). These were expected to speak for the good of God's people in the context of spiritual development for sustainable living. This Scripture does not focus on a particular leadership but all leadership mandated to lead and guide God's people. The church cannot speak from the pulpit the message of saving souls only without the message of saving the rest of God's creation, for the mandate is very clear as given in Genesis chapter one: 'So that they may rule' (Gen.1:26). This is where the theology of work and development becomes relevant, to address challenges caused by development that might not be life- long sustainable. Most of the development programs undertaken are for the benefits of individuals or companies. Most of the communities in the areas where development programs takes place, usually walk out with nothing, or become affected by the expansions and residual deposits from industries or factories. At the back of our minds, we must ask ourselves; what kind of development are people engaged in? How does such development benefit the people and how does it support life? Sustainability is not only an economic dimension, but also a social and religious human concern that involves animal and plant life longevity since humanity cannot live in isolation from the rest of creation. When a government is constructing a road to last for fifty years, she must also plan for people that are going to be served by the same road to see that they can outlive the road's life span. However, some of environmental impact assessment might have been left out. Nevertheless, if they have ever been done, greedy and selfish people might have sidelined them, because the visible truth is that most people suffer displacement, property destruction, disease and even death at the expense of infrastructural developments. The first pictures illustrate the environmental degradation that has already started to affect the echo system negatively. God did not give us the earth to develop it for a limited period of time but rather for as long as human life exists. Human life does not start and end with us today but is a continuation of generations, far in history and beyond the present into the future. True generations come and go but the earth remains. Each generations' responsibility is to work towards sustaining the next generations beyond time and space. It is important to think, work and live within a sustainable development. No matter where one is, the responsibility is with each one of us.

II

DEVELOPMENTAL CONCEPTS

Development is a concept of progress. It begins with planning in the head and then on paper. If the concept is wrongly conceived, even the paper work for practical purposes will be corrupt. The eyes of many are not keen enough to understand where faults lie because they are mostly lay eyes. It is not after the concept has been approved and put on ground that the effects begin to surface, and in some cases, the law is not protective of individual losses. With such developments, the unfortunate thing has been to minimize them to socio-economic development only, where even the economic is more pronounced than the social. The rest might come as an afterthought. Therefore, to make meaningful development, it may carry different dimensions based on which aspect of engagement it is addressing. For example, the concept of physical development is different from that one of social or spiritual development. However, it makes great sense if we tried as much as possible to marry all the dimensions and their concepts together in order to paint a picture of a holistic development; for human beings in their work life tend to interact with all of them for their living, but mostly for the service of God. Whatever an individual does in respect of personal development, must be measured within the public interest because in the end there is no development that serves individuals without affecting others since individuals exist in the interest of their societies. That is why our development plans must address the material and the spiritual good. In his book; *Economic Development,* Todaro says that development is.

A multi-dimensional process should be involved including major changes in social structures as well as the acceleration of economic growth, the reduction of inequality and the eradication of poverty. Development, in its essence, must represent the whole gamut of change by which an entire social system moves away from a condition of life widely perceived as unsatisfactory towards a situation or condition of life regarded as materially and spiritually better[7].

If major social changes are to be realized, the Christian behind the wheel that turns the industry of life must think in the direction of the whole range of change from within to the outer world. The church to which the Christians subscribe their membership should be very much concerned about those who are engaged in developmental work and help them not to engage meaningless development if it misses the concept of sustainability which Todaro has called entire social system (that) moves away from a condition of life widely perceived as unsatisfactory.

6. Moving Towards Sustainability

The two terms: "work" and "development" are very much related because in development, there is no work that is destructive and there is no work without developmental impact. Talking of development, we are really having in mind the idea of growth in size, quality and progression. It might be social, physical, spiritual, economic, political or even mental growth, which must be fundamentally visible with models and outcomes. There is no way we can look at development outside the context of work, and we should know that work derives its holistic meaning from the theological perspective of creation. This means that work and development must underscore the religious importance of our mandate. In this case, development and work are considered as both academic and

---

[7] Todaro, M.P, *Economic Development* (Essex: Pearson Educational Limited, 2000), p.18.

religious disciplines that help us understand our calling through "the study of God and his creation" but also not forgetting its sociological aspect. Work and development are manifestations of God's presence. When we see the works of creation, it is surrounded by God's power and glory, but also it emanates from God himself. See figure 1 below

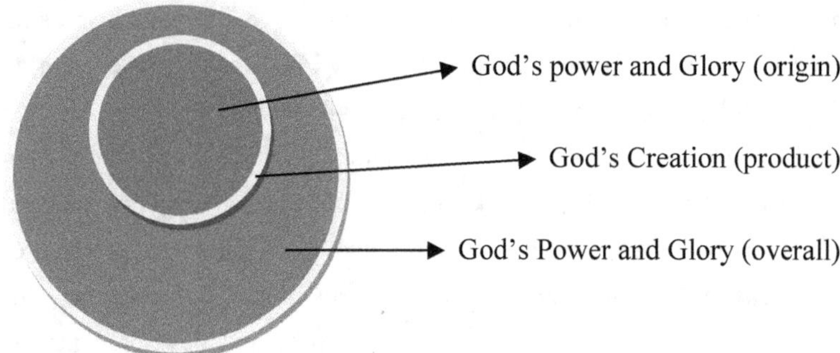

Figure 1: Showing God's creation, power and Glory.

This implies that work is under the control of God the author and perfector. There is no way one can imagine having control over what is not in his or her own mandate. Moreover, we are part of the created works of God but with the ability to use other created order. Our real mandate is to use God's created works for secondary works of development purposely for our own benefits but in accordance to the laid out divine pattern. In this case, development work is 'from God, by God and for God'. No more, no less. Nothing done outside these three walls is for development.

Besides, development being an academic discipline, theological disciplines must be acknowledged as studies of religion and beliefs or sets of religious beliefs[8] from which we develop our understanding of God and his creation. Theology from the religious point of view portrays God

---

[8] A.S Hornby, *Oxford Advanced Learner's Dictionary*, sixth ed. (Oxford: Oxford University Press, 2004), p.1400.

through the wondrous environment, which is his developed work, and this is where our primary assignment was designed for life. That is why the Bible among 'many other religious sacred Scriptures' plays an important role in teaching people about God, work and development. Biblical theology therefore according to Wayne Grudem "should be explicitly based on the teachings of Scriptures…, where the Bible gives support for the doctrines under consideration"[9] and one of the major doctrines so much neglected is the "doctrine of work" which is being addressed here. Grudem's statement is very important in understanding that work and development are theological aspects of human life that guide us within the given environment and that they must be taught from the Biblical perspective. Work and development give people special attention to the teaching of scriptures and understanding the place of each teaching in the historical development of the environment. This implies that when studying Theology of work and development, the Bible becomes one of the best resources for environmental and sustainable development. God, in his eternal wisdom knew how humanity was to deal with the environment and he instructed; "to subdue and replenish it" (Gen.1:28), and this instruction was an assurance of sustaining development. The Biblical understanding of subduing the earth connotes getting rid of such impediments that might stand in the way of developing the environment, but also we can advance it farther by calling upon each one of us to develop our mental capacities in order to meet the developmental goals of our environment. The theology of development looks beyond the present to the future, far away from our present time. It has a long-range focus and the theology of replenishing is suggestive of continuity of life by renewing and replacing the degraded or over used environment. Development must not be one-sided aspect, by looking at building infrastructure like roads, and industries, which are necessary for contributing to the economic sustainability. We must not ignore the

---

[9] Wayne Grudem, *Systematic Theology* (Leicester, England: IVP, 2000), p.15.

respect for the natural environment like forests, swamps, rivers and others that support the wellbeing of mankind, animals and plants; because all of them greatly depend on this natural environment as their habitat, besides supporting conducive climate for all. Infrastructure without human beings is meaningless and anti-human. If we look at the earlier pictures, we will be able to understand that infrastructural development often tends to degrade the natural environment, and displaces other habitats like wild life and even human beings. It must be noted that when the green cover is replaced with any kind of infrastructure, it will never come back forever. In most cases infrastructure dominates the original essence of development as described by the Scriptures. Eventually, the infrastructural development planners will have no more plans because they will have already destroyed the natural environment that the future will need.

When there is too much of economic, activity that seeks to increase financial benefits on the expense of social life it will also affect the spiritual life of the people because spirituality is an all-encompassing life value of what we do or do not do. If we disregard it, then the key role of the environment that was entrusted to us becomes meaningless and more degraded, and eventually a less important economic player. As a result, the same environment will fail to sustain and support any farther economic activity. It will become very expensive to rejuvenate the environment in order to have it respond to real productivity. However, the idea of replenishing becomes very important, when the environment is no longer providing optimum human needs like in agriculture and health. We must understand that every day that passes; it increases the human life the earth can efficiently accommodate or optimally support. However, when we fail to relate human population to the environmental efficacy, the whole purpose of creation loses value. God did not create a small world for us, but because of our becoming too ambitious and selfish, seeking far more than we need as individuals, denying others opportunities to live happily, including animals and plants; the world has become too small for us and at the same time a place of struggling. In so doing we begin to move away from our apportioned places, and we begin displacing and destroying our neighbors and neighborhood.

In the current situation where demand is higher than supply, people will find all excuses to create different avenues, no matter the effects, to make sure that they meet the market demand. That is why there is a very high degree of environmental degradation, displacement, disturbance and destruction. The cause might sound economically reasonable to move very first and innovatively, but sometimes the eyes set on satisfying the market demands might overlook the sustainability components. In that case, the development goals must consider many factors other than the market demand. Our land must be retuned and restructured by means of innovations that are favorable to global concerns. Sustainability is a long-term perspective that must defy a number of odds for the sake of its enthusiasts. Any development must be pro creation and especially to the environment in order to bring about sustainability not only locally but also globally. Therefore, work and development being a process of boundless engagement must recognize that the environment has to go through a process that can address global concerns. Roads, railways, airports and oil industries' constructions in most cases have been the mostly destructive much as they are key players in social and economic developments of nations. Road construction for example uses materials like marram, stones and land. There is no way how it will avoid hills and valleys, swamps and forests. This is very necessary because if we want to preserve environment then we must forget development. Nevertheless, if we want to put up sustainable development, we must be very innovative and creative and see how best we can avoid mega degradation and destruction of our environment as in picture no.3, otherwise we will need it when it will no longer be there at all. Looking at the picture no.4 below, you will be able to see the destructive impact of stone quarries on humanity and the environment, not forgetting all other life.

Picture 4: stone quarrying

Eliza S. Miles says that quarrying to the environment is very evident because there is; visual intrusion, damage to landscapes, traffic, smoke, noise, dust, damage to caves, loss of land, and a deterioration in water quality.

The best understanding of the sustainable development process then will always depend on God's revelation, and develop theories to explain their beliefs in God. People's beliefs and practices must fall within the practical and biblical theologies that will become the means, by which they can attempt to understand God as a principle developer. This can help people especially the church to understand her role in the revealed world of work. In addition, Biblical theology should help people understand how to explain God's relationship with his people and creation through the Scriptures. To talk of sustainable development, the church must first understand how she can engage in development herself; the type of development that does not violet the theology of work and people's spiritual, social, economic and health wellbeing, because her mandate in the world of work is to be a steward of God's creation. Irrespective of what type of development is undertaken, people must have integrative theories so that at no point should development become a one sided aspect. In our developmental plans, we must avoid revolutionary economic gains that bring about environmental negative impact where there will be excessive use of the resources or imbalanced industrialization and utility of resources. In the book; *Sustainable Development; Economics and Environment in the Third World,* the authors expressed that; What we do now affects the future, regardless of the fact that we do not know who future people will be, confers rights on future generation; and the truth is that we are enjoying the past heritage left by our predecessors. It could be argued out that the past had no pressing economic and social demands like it is today, but still we could tell from the extent of their environmental engagements of that time. This therefore becomes relevant of what Robert asserts that; "Sustainability means that long-term perspectives (which) should apply to all policies and actions, with sustainable well-being and sustainable livelihood as objects for present and future generations."[10] Any development that puts humanity at the periphery will end in complete turmoil. Work geared towards development will always have in focus of the 'future' and that is why an environmental impact assessment is a very important aspect especially in industrial and urban development so that it does not lose its purpose for the common good of the present and future generations. In Australia, the white settlers and the development of cities displaced the indigenous people: the Aborigines, who have ever since lived like wild animals, yet were, and are human like all others. Human life is determined by generations from which they come. The development we are always concerned with is partially to serve our present generation's interest; other-

---

[10] Robert Chambers, *Ideas for Development* (London: Earthscan, 2005), p.193.

wise, most of it is intended to serve the next generations. If that were the case, we should always be mindful of what development we are engaged in and what type of environment we are dealing with.

From a Christian point of view therefore, we must see the importance of environmental and developmental assessment before we embark on any developmental projects. The church should not distance herself from taking responsibility of interpreting the biblical teaching to all those who engage in physical development so that the world can remain a haven of peace for everyone living on it.

Most desired developments destroy mostly desired environment. Mega developments like construction of Airports, Rail lines, Continental road infrastructures, Oil drilling and refineries are mostly desired projects but they cannot fail to destroy the most desired environment. It is very important to note that no matter of what importance and magnitude development might be; it must never ignore the spiritual value if it has to be able to address the whole life of human kind. Development therefore of any magnitude should never overlook the importance and contribution of the church as the divine voice meant to give counsel on matters of human and environmental importance. However, the question that comes to us is, Does the church have the expertise to direct such developmental issues? The answer is yes, because she has the likes of Cyrus, Solomon, and Nehemiah who were just political leaders but were used by God to do his work for his people. The spiritual perspective in development is therefore more primary than all other aspects in development for God speaks and directs human activities through the church. This does not overlook all other religions provided they advocate for the same with a similar emphasis. Believe me or not, development that does not consider the importance of human and the environment there of, is not sustainable. This is evident where most of the development in most of the countries has taken very large forest cover and as a result, there are many climatic negative changes affecting life on land and water bodies.

God in his wisdom, created countries with large coverage of thick or dense forests while others were created with large coverage of dry sand deserts. The thick forests were intended to provide what dry sand deserts could not provide for their people. When we destroy such vegetation, we deny other people living in most disadvantaged countries to enjoy life in many ways. People of the world though separated by natural or political borders, they are co-existent and interdependent. Therefore, as we mind about the development of our nations, we should know that in many ways we affect others directly or indirectly, positively or negatively as we do to our own people.

Therefore understanding the Scriptures would help us address such issues threatening the existence of human life and its surrounding thereon, on the expense of development. Scholars, who are not Christians, need not fear reading the Bible as one of the major sources of information when dealing with human life and development. Let the Bible be the main and most important manual on any development engagements and the best literature for informing all concepts regarding sustainable development. If the Quran has material to address the developmental issues, read it even if you are not a Muslim. The earlier we understand what development involves the better; for a stitch in time saves a nine[11].

7. The Participation of the Church in Sustainable Development

The place of Church's participation in the world of work and sustainable development is not only based on the weight of its numbers, but has also to do with the understanding of what happens in the Gospel

---

[11] Francis Baily, *Journal of a Tour in Unsettled Parts of North America* (Published by Augustus Morgan, 1856).

influenced minds since she has received the Gospel and sought to appropriate it in her context.[12] This makes it very relevant therefore to know that Christians have an important role in integrating their faith with their work in order to maintain an environment for sustainable development and mitigate the false impressions of the church's exclusion as a non-development player.

The church therefore must endeavor to identify the roles she can play within the environment they live in order to register sustainable development based on biblical theology of work. It has not been easy to mobilize Christians and Church leaders today towards marketplace ministry due to minimum understanding of the theology of work[13]. This has become a short coming mainly because environmental and developmental matters are rarely discussed within churches, but only as casual subjects without any particular emphasis of the advantages and disadvantages of knowledge or lack of it to achieving local and global sustainable development. The church leaders are therefore called upon, to study and master the theology of development, so that they can share it with the developers. There are specific themes that speak out directly or indirectly which would make sense if environmental and sustainable development were to be looked at from a global face factor. These would include the theology of creation, redemption, and eschatology. Without undermining the importance of all other beliefs, Christians can play a very important role to affect the environment based on those themes. Bediako asserts that: "The church is called to infuse the world with hope, for both this age and the next".[14] These themes are not just for Christians' spiritual purpose but also for all humanity to understand their importance in

---

[12] Kwame Bediako, *Christianity in Africa: The Renewal of a non-Western Religion* (USA: Orbis Books, 1997), p.128-9.

[13] Paul Stevens and Alvin Ung, *Taking Your Soul To Work* (USA: Eerdmans, 2009), p.2.

[14] Samuel Vinay and Sugden Chris, *The Church in Response to Human Need.* (Grand Rapids: Eerdmans, Regnum Books, 1987), p.24.

the world that supplies our human needs. People should understand the importance of integrating what they know with what they do based on the taught biblical truth to be able to impact development. In the Great Commission, Jesus instructed his Disciples to go and 'teach'. Without doubt, most of the Christian Churches have done more of preaching on the expense of teaching. This has resulted into failure of acquiring knowledge about many important life matters like environmental and developmental ethics, which could closely relate with the Puritan work ethic developed in the 16th and 17th century in England. Because of this failure, human beings, the artisans of development or progression have now become ignorant and the most endangered of the species, by them-selves. Unless teaching takes its place among God's people, for sure sustainable development will never come. In Hosea, of course from a spiritual point of view, God says; "My people are perishing for lack of knowledge" (Hos.4:6). This can also apply in other areas of human life. Ignorance is one of the key factors to a slow but sure death if not dealt with through sharing experiences of other nations around us. Teaching is one of the elements that aims at avoiding ignorance and bringing trans-formations, changing the mind set of those who are engaged in destruc-tive development, making them to grow and live in faith, for "We can-not overestimate the importance of the edification of God's people through regular and systematic teaching and preaching of the word."[15] Unless we engage the world of work and development, where teaching becomes as important as preaching and they both become our prime core values of transformation, the environment will disappear at our own hands while we watch as we disappear at the same time. Education has brought the world where it is now, although the misuse of knowledge has led to degradation of the environment in the name of developing

---

[15] Derek Prime, *Pastors and Teachers: A Calling and Work of Christ's Under-shepherds* (United Kingdom: Christian Books for Africa and Asia 'Southside, 2004), p.12.

science and technology to which sustainable development players must check the extent of their positive or negative effects. Science and technology should not be looking at discoveries and innovations of what we use, but also at how human life can be innovated to cope up with new technological challenges.

Theology of work is the source of market place ministry, a Mission field where Church and all other people do their work, take God's presence and influence the work they do with their spirituality. Bediako has also observed that; "Even if God's activity is focused on the church, it is not confined to the church. God's particular focus on the church as on Israel in the Old Testament- has as its purpose the blessing of the nations. Thus the church is called to exist for the sake of its Lord and for the sake of humankind."[16] In other words, the church is not the sole player, but one of the avenues God has used to communicate his intentions for his creation. The Church therefore, must see her workplaces as God's estate, where her work will have positive impact. When Jesus Christ promises; "I am with you always…" (Mtt.28:20), it means that in our work places where we spend most of our life time, irrespective of what services we offer to God, we are not working alone. Therefore, the Church is called upon to work for and with God to make meaningful development, least her efforts are wasted (Ps.127). In this case, the Theology of work is an endeavor to engage in the mission of God, which long began at creation (Gen.1:26-28; 2:15). This is where the Father exists and works in relationship to the Son and the Holy Spirit, revealing one another and bringing characteristic emphasis to sustain the environment and its development. Any development that has no future generations in focus is a meaningless and destructive development. God, aware of what human beings were capable of doing, he made it very clear on two counts. (i) To replenish the environment (Gen.1:28) and, (ii) to tend and keep it (Gen.2:15).

---

[16] Bediako, p.143.

To understand the importance of sustainable development, all people but more especially Christians need to identify themselves with the biblical patterns of development within the window of positive revolution rather than the window of distortion. God had created man in completeness (Gen.1:26) but disobedience destroyed all the goodness in humankind, thus rendering work and development controlled by hardships. The idea of; 'subduing the environmental hazards and replenishing the depleted environment was overlooked because development has tended to seek selfish ends more than universal good. The redeeming work of Christ was not intended for only humankind but all creation for the final glory that the second coming of Jesus Christ will bring. However, one of the dominant themes will be on the fall, because it is the fall; that has corrupted everything, almost to the point of no redemption, except through Jesus Christ.

The theology of the fall is very important in guiding us why things are not the way God had intended them to be. The fall brings in our environment the concept of failure and lack of reviewing our way back. God in his wisdom however did not abandon humankind, but instead provided redemptive measures from the fall (Gen.3:21), with an aim of not redeeming humankind only, but work too. This became a process through which mankind could regain the former glory, and where finally mankind would become liberated from the fall and all of God's work would resume as was intended, and the culmination of this process would be 'Consummation' or making complete, where God's creation would revert to its intended position.

In one factory where poultry feeds were being processed, workers faced a problem of no payment for some months and yet the factory was functional. It was reported that one of the disappointed workers decided to mix the required ingredients in a disproportional measurement and the product failed most of the farmers. It was not until a veterinary expert was called and proved that the feeds were corrupted. All the stock had to be condemned and thorough supervision undertaken to have a better product out. This example is intended to tell us that corrupted work cannot be overlooked and be allowed to continue because its effects will affect us the consumers. There are many people out there who do not care about what they produce out of their work and yet God took all the care when he was creating them (See the creation work in Genesis 1&2). The Scriptures tell us that we are wonderfully and fearfully made (Ps.139:14). This would equally be interpreted into the wonderful work that must come out of our hearts, minds and hands.

III

CREATIVE WORK
FOR SUSTAINABLE DEVELOPMENT

Creation is God's work that brought everything in existence and he gave humankind the creative skills to be part of his creation by displaying God given skills to produce works of innovation and inspiration. God bestowed on humankind special abilities through his image and likeness. He gave them wisdom or rationale to be creative and even engage positively what was placed before them. God's creation is a self-based wisdom that though humankind was given the wisdom to co-create and procreate, they cannot equate their wisdom with that of God, and cannot share in equal measure with God. This means that when dealing with issues of development, we must be aware that we have limitations to recreate much as we are given God's wisdom. We cannot make development that can stand the test of time. Whatever we do here on earth is limited by time and value. It has an end. This calls for an intellectual and theological application of what we have been assigned to for our sustainability. While the creative skill has been ascribed to humankind for the assigned work, Chewing says; "creativity is a core concept for artistic production…seen as an especially gifted visionary of spiritual truth"[17] In this respect, when God created, he created order

---

[17] R. C. Chewing writes in the *Dictionary of Christian Ethics and Pastoral Theology* about *creation ethics* and points out on the core concept of creation ethics. He says this concept is related to producing art, which is reality in putting

from a chaotic world in an artistic manner (Gen.1:1). That kind of development has sustained the universe from rudimentary to superior status. In the same way Grudem says; "God allowed significant measures of skill in artistic... areas, as well as in other spheres in which creativity and skill can be expressed..."[18] Creation therefore bares much of God's own intellect and artwork and it is supposed to be eternal, just as God is eternal. In the world of work and development, the Church has the ability and responsibility to work with in the defined work patterns controlled by God's intellect, and for that matter; the church can become the change agent of positive development. In the book of Genesis.1:26, the image and likeness determine how human beings should be God like to determine the level of their engagement in development. This overshadows the economic benefits thereof or the remuneration concept to what we earn or do as part of our work engagements.

In Gen.2:7, the breathing into man's nostrils the breath of life was the divine way of giving man ability to function God like. The breath of life represents God's spirit that makes human beings what they are. Every Christian must learn and understand the theology of being created in the image and likeness of God. Men are not made to appear like monuments of creation but to be the pinnacle of creation representing the highest of God's artwork and intellect and these must be manifested in their active presence at, and in their work. This means that in order to realize sustainable development, we must engage our hands, heads and hearts that God gave us purposely for his service work in developing our resources for our sustainability. The human work mechanism can be explained by the figure below, where the heart is the sole mover, send-

---

abilities to work. He says that looking back to the 17th and 18th centuries, humankind sought to emancipate itself from created cosmos governed by divine law where they replaced it with the creative power of the human mind.

[18] Grudem, p.661.

ing the messages to the head and the head interprets them into what other parts of the body can do.

8. The Wheels of Work Industry

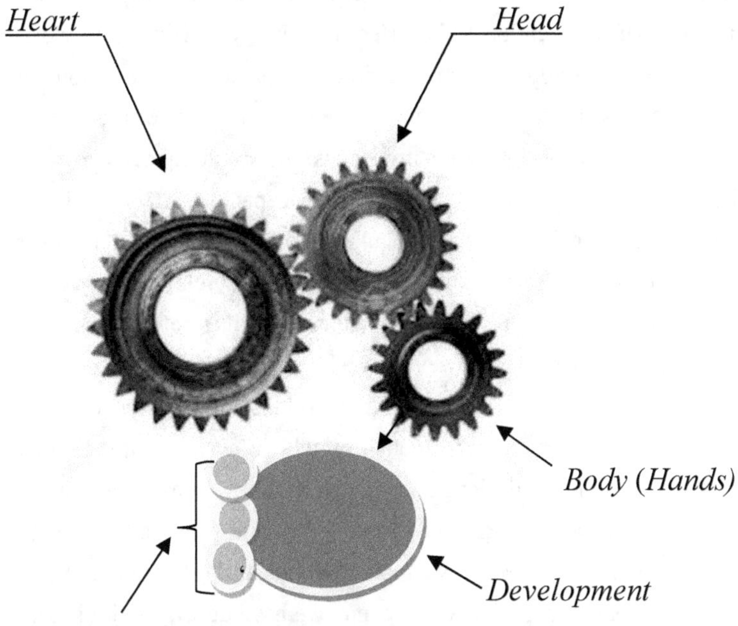

Fig 2: The interrelation between the heart, the head and the hands

God gave part of his abilities to humankind for their own sake to be able to develop and earn a living out of their environment. The Bible without mincing up words speaks clearly of how Jesus Christ revealed God (Jn.17:6; Cor.1:15) Christians' work is to maintain form and order in a world of work that had been corrupted and its values degraded, if sustainable development is to be a reality. God has given human beings his spirit to create (Gen.1:26-28). Every human being is of God, by God and in God. This is evident and can be seen in many different ways where human beings are involved in a wide range of craftsmanship such as pottery, weaving, planning, plumbing and many others (See Ex. 31:3-6).The advantage of the church is that her biblical resources pronounce human responsibilities in the world more than any other resources available. Therefore, the church is not only designed for specific artisanship, but also with special abilities derived from Jesus Christ, who has liberated her and all the creation to be effectively influential in the world of work, without overlooking the principles of sustainable development. The biblical clearly tells us that one of the characteristics of God's likeness in humankind is intellect. Intellect is an inbuilt capacity to think and do things guided by God given mental capacities. It is a spiritual incentive that God has put in humankind with great abilities to allow them to think and work for a better world. It is very relevant to ask ourselves questions like: Why, how or what and the alike before we engage our developmental work. However, we know that the fall of man destroyed the great abilities of thinking and working for a better world. We are like someone cutting a tree branch on which he/she is sitting. What would have sustained life longer has been reduced so much and disregarded for the benefits of greedy people today, and when today is gone, we cannot be sure of tomorrow. Instead of sustaining the environment for ourselves, and the generation to come, we have destroyed, it thinking that we are innovatively improving its capacity to sustain life. Therefore, the coming of Christ becomes the hope to restore the lost abilities because when we become Christians, our thinking and doing things change for the better. We become the manifestations of the redeemed world and its work and the outcome is strategic and sustainable development. If all people took the biblical teaching seriously, without doubt the Eden Paradise would be restored and people would deal with the environment more honestly (cf. Gen2:15), and profitably for today and tomorrow.

However, because humankind has kept on wavering, the Bible declares that God will come once and shake the Heaven's and the Earth and all the nations (Hag.2:6) and create a new heaven and earth

(Rev.21). In that case, the focus must change form specific to general, from Christians to all humankind and we cannot underrate that caution because that Scripture tells us that God will bring restoration to all. Our concern therefore is not limited to Christians but to all people engaged in critical developmental work. They need to know where we have come from, where we are and where we are going. The effects of development whether positive or negative defy cultural, racial or religious boundaries. The world that Jim Reeves sang about as not being our home has indeed proved not to be, but unfortunately, many of us have made it our permanent and final destination. This has come because of our failed responsibilities to maintaining form and order for sustainable development. Whatever we are doing, seem to suggest that we are here forever without seeing how rapidly the environment is disappearing with its occupants. Conscious of the final restatement of God's creation in Revelation.21:5, if work entrusted to humankind had maintained order and form, there would have been no need for making all things new. Christians who read and believe in the Bible must take this as a very thoughtful matter because responsibility to God's work lies in their hearts, heads and hands. They must participate in God's creation and even be creative in the world of work. Their presence and impact need to be felt wherever the church works or serves. A church needs to remind her members of why they should work or how and when to work. When Christ revealed himself, the why, how and when became very clear to Christians in their everyday life. Christian developers who are distorting the values of development, must be avoided and carefully counseled, otherwise they are betraying, and undermining the practical mission of their church.

9. Faulty Human Efforts

Biblical understanding of the fall of man is a historical occurrence, not a purported story. The story of the Bible tells us that man made an effort in being like God and in the process; he went far away from him by losing that close relationship he used to enjoy. Thinking through the inquiry when God called; "where are you?" (Gen.3:9), we can see God's concern about the lost value of relationship. We do not know what God was going to do this time round, but we know that true relationship is never limited to ideas. Adam's absence from his rightful place of work, caused him lose God's confidence and he lost all that belonged to him. God did not ask Adam as if he did not know what he had done, but wanted Adam to be aware of God's prior knowledge of Adams failure to keep his place. This affected Adam's wellbeing and capacity to make reasonable decisions for the best option, instead he hid away from his responsibilities, and ever since it has remained a burden to mankind (Gen.3:17-19). Whatever work in development we experience, it is horizontal rather than being vertical. *Sometimes it is neither vertical nor horizontal but a scribble* and then ends rotating around self (self-serving and appraising, see fig. below).

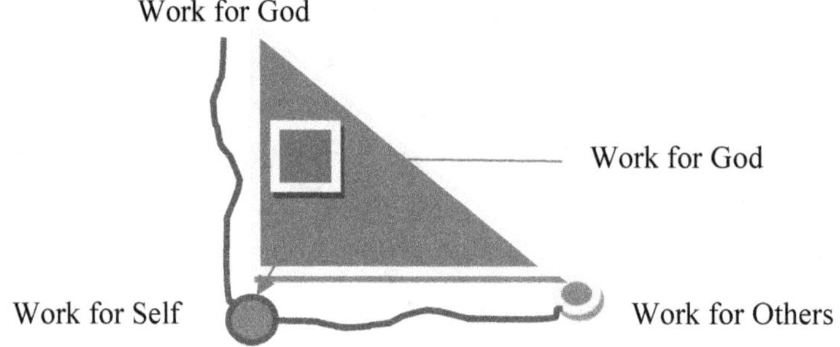

Figure 3: Showing man's reality of work.

This has remained the greatest fault that has ever affected all creation including the earth where we work as the Bible says; "the ground is cursed because of you. All your life you will struggle to scratch a living from it." (Gen.3:17c). No one thinks about what others need for a living, instead each person thinks of "self" not even the creator; thus a non-vertical approach.

The fall is caused by a fault which might be more of internal than external problem. It is a spiritual matter, deep seated in people's hearts. Adam knew very well from his fellowship what God had told him. He knew it by heart, and must have shared it with his wife Eve from time to time. The failure of the heart and the brain were the source of the fall. This is where Christian faith brings about not only spiritual regeneration but also a potential change of lifestyle and motivation.[19] Human fault is internal and inherent bringing guilt and shame, because of its deep-rooted effects, which keep on destroying the work and development values. Even when well knowing the benefits of sustainable development, most of the search for economic satisfaction has overlooked and overtaken the importance of environmental contribution and the lack of impact assessment. Pearce and colleagues say that; "the environmental impact assessment procedure is important in order to identify the monetary cost of resources and the receiving environmental damage"[20]. What we think to be development using our human capacities is sometimes short of God's expectations because it is always self- seeking. Whenever we engage work, we expect monetary profits that cannot be fulfilled. Work without economic benefits, is never referred to as work by most people. Most of the people will go out to try all possible means to get the best out of their environment with no regard to the negative outcomes. What cannot be denied is that the created order no longer directly correspond to the 'goodness' (Gen.1:31) of its original form. It was bleached, but it is redeemable through the doctrine of salvation (redemption/restoration). In his article '*Christian Reconstruction Movement*', Child says; "By forcing Christians to grapple with the Old Testament's

---

[19] J. N. Hall's article; "Development of Spirituality*",* In the *New Dictionary of Christian Ethics & Pastoral Theology*. Edited by David J. Atkinson and David H. Field (England: Inter Varsity Press, 1995), pp.463-64.

[20] David Pearce, Edward Barbier and Anil Markandya, *Sustainable Development. Economic and Environment in the Third World* (London: Earthscan Publishers, 1990), p.47.

contribution to Christian ethics and just society, and by offering insightful biblical solutions to the problems of the modern world, the Reconstructionists have enriched the church."[21] Implying that the Church has the capacity to reconstruct the degraded environmental patterns for the sake of sustainable development and change the problems facing the world of work and the development thereof. There is a hope kept alive in the theology and spirituality of the monastic work tradition where the Benedictine monasticism expressed the idea of the unique characteristic of a strong rule of work ethic, for each Monk was assigned as a must, to do manual labor every day. It is reported that, with the feudal social structure of the middle ages, the work of God became regular in form of prayers and Psalter recitation and became exclusively spiritual.[22] Therefore, Biblical theology of work helps Christians to construct a Christian theology of work and development from spiritual perspective. It helps them to look back from where they have come to where they are going, so that the present can take a better advantage of its development to what the future theology of work would be. What we do now affects the future, irrespective of who will be there then and how many. This sends a clear message that we are enjoying the rich heritage left by our predecessors. The message of the Bible is not static. Its theology is so dynamic that the bible remains the foundation for sustainable development of all generations in spite of the changing situations. Therefore, the Christian church ought not to blend with the corrupt world, because she has the spirit of God. Instead of blending with the world, she should be transformational in nature. However, throughout all generations the fall has remained the major threat to perfection of work and development to

---

[21] J. G. Child, (1995) in his article: "Christian Reconstruction" in: *The New Dictionary of Christian Ethics and Pastoral Studies* (Nottingham, England: IVP, 1995), p.227.

[22] T. O. Kay, in his article; "Monasticism" in: *The New Dictionary of Christian Ethics and Pastoral Studies* (Nottingham, England: IVP, 1995), p.598.

the extent that even church leaders have been caught up in web of failure. That is why most of the people engaged in church work first think about how much they are to gain financially more than what their ministry responsibilities are.

10. Irresponsible Church Leadership

Of recent in Uganda many people including churches have turned to swamps and natural forests and made them into animal and agricultural farmlands. Some churches have used swamps to plant Eucalyptus trees, which trees have been scientifically proven to drain water tables and catchment areas.

Picture 5: Showing the dried swamp after planting eucalyptus trees.

The swamp after eucalyptus trees have been planted and grown up, the water is drained leaving the land dry. (Examples of this type can be found on most of the church land in West Ankole Diocese: Bweranyangi church land, South Ankole Diocese: Kitunga Archdeaconry land and Ankole Diocese: Kinono Archdeaconry land, all found in South Western Uganda)

To the people and their leaders, they are looking at the short-term profits to be generated from the trees without seeing the negative effects on weather caused by the destruction of swamps and drained water catchments. This is one of the many examples where the church as a body is engaged as part of developmental projects because most of the churches have been encouraged to plant eucalyptus trees as a means of generating income. In some other cases some churches do commercial brick making and they call it long lasting money-generating project. The longer it lasts, the more it degrades the environment, leaving long lasting negative environmental impact.

11. Negative Environmental Impact of the Church

Picture 6: Brick making project by some Christians and church institutions for generating family and church income

One of the questions that may come to the reader's mind is; how can the church become a voice for, and engage in sustainable development when she is herself engaged in degrading activities? The church is one among many other institutions that has a big following. If she engaged her members into positive and sustainable development right from the grass root (family level) to the institutional level, she would have realized the primary role of her ministry both in the local and global sustainable development. Her voice is the motherly voice calling for the sincerity and meaning of life through development. It does matter a lot what we call income generating project, especially when we think about life sustaining projects not in terms of money, but in terms of social and spiritual wellbeing for the people present today and tomorrow.

Therefore, the above are a few examples that affect the climatic conditions that reverse the general crop productivity and climatic seasonal changes in the country. Human beings, animals and plants; all become adversely affected. Some people, who have encroached on the most important swamps and natural forests for their personal benefits, have instead asked the government to compensate them for the development already done in swamps and forest. Without shame of having destroyed the weather and climatic cycle, they want to cause another financial damage to the taxpayers' money by asking for compensation. This has of late been evident in mostly affected parts of Uganda where rich people engaging in crop and animal faming have claimed big chunks of private and public land. We cannot be surprised that many of them are Christians[23]. We cannot blame them because the theology of environment and sustainable development for sure has not been clearly manifested in the Christian teaching about their creation mandate. The government leaders are as well ignorant of the realities of environmental degradation. Those who have the knowledge have been influenced by greed to capitalize on the ignorance of many. It is therefore very unfor-

---

[23] Many prominent Christians in Western Uganda destroyed a big acreage of swamps to develop cattle farms. It is now about forty years since, and the government having failed to remove them, many other farmers have started to do the same.

tunate that sometimes Christians do not stretch their mental map to see how far the fall has affected them and the world around them, and how best the church can renew their thinking as they engage in their everyday work.

However, the church has many ways in which she can affect her members as well as the world of work around them. To maintain God's good work and rational development we need total commitment, effort, quality time and equity. The church builds a unique character in her members as well as the society where she belongs because her participation and work values are highly regarded in real development and if applied they can bring the centrality of God in her work engagements to please God and to be rewarded. Today's corruption surrounding work is a serious replica of the failed Eden family life because we no longer listen to God instead we listen to ourselves, and those around us. We are influenced by greed, anxiety and sometimes jealousy. Even the Christians who confess Christ as their personal savior, when faced with the moral decadence at workplaces, they find it easy to conform and blend, leaving no opportunity for identity. We cannot doubt that a good percentage of the politicians are Christians,[24] besides being business developers. In the practical terms of development, they are seen as best performers, but we know that most of the perpetrators of degenerating environment and corrupted development come from the world of politicians and business developers. Surprisingly, these people will do their best to shut doors against those who preach sanity and transformation in politics and business development. One of the most negative influences on our environment is the urbanization and agricultural shifts[25] because these

---

[24] According to *Wikipedia* the 10th Parliament of 2016-2021, the Muslim parliamentarians is at approximately 6.7%, leaving an assumed Christian percentage of 93.3%. (accessed 29/09/2018)

[25] Cf. *New Vision*, 28/09/2018, p. 9, under the heading "Wetlands disappearing faster than forests-conservationists".

two are spreading rapidly like a wild fire replacing and displacing vital environment in the name of development. The truth is that as long as swamps and forests disappear, the eco system will greatly change affecting all life. This is not to say that development should be stopped, but it is to suggest that there must be mechanisms for keeping life worth living as it had been without excessive negative impact. This implies that today's urbanization and agricultural plans are not conducive for sustainable development. Besides using a lot of scientific researches and control experiments, the truth cannot be overlooked that they have instead increased life threats to humanity and its environment. However, as said earlier, the Bible has the best perspective on how to utilize our environment for sustainable development and the church as God's institution has the mandate to declare that truth to herself and others.

That means that the biblical doctrine of redemption is not a divorced truth from politics and business world. The majority of people who sit behind the church pews on Sundays and the following morning fill the marketplace stalls or offices of Organizations and political positions know the truth but rarely apply it. We cannot say that Christian values are only applicable in the church and not in the marketplace, no! Only that the church has not come out boldly to share the truth with the world around her because some church leaders have become part of the world around them and as such they may not have the moral courage to denounce developmental negative concerns. Unless the church leaders disassociate themselves from unsustainable engagements, the world will continue at a pace faster than it has been before because the likely advocates for sustainable development have turned against it. The questions Like who is in the marketplace, who is involved in developing ideas and skills, who are those people who have no moral obligations to recognize, reorganize and protect the environment for sustaining development seem never to appeal to anybody. The church will not have carried out her universal mission from a holistic viewpoint if she appeared static, meaningless and dormant institution. Nevertheless, what is well known is that the church is a living organ that moves and lives with us. Therefore, whatever Christians hear and share in the church must form the basis or fundamentals of every development.

Truth is not only relevant on Sunday and irrelevant from Monday to Saturday. We are the same who sit in the churches that are in the marketplace. The seeds of morality are planted or sown on Sunday, and they instantly grow into fruits visible right from Monday when people go to their workplaces. Everyday including Sunday that follow, the preacher prunes and weeds out destructive weeds and work life continues for the better. That is how Christian life is lived and the Church moves from inside the individual and the building walls to the marketplace. Development therefore begins from within an individual.

Whatever the case might be, individual negative responses to the plight of environmental issues affect sustainability and productivity that eventually undermine development globally. Global warming that has affected the climatic changes is a contribution of almost everyone in one way or the other regardless of the level of the contribution. It has not allowed many to see and keep to terms with the ideals of how to realize sustainable development. Values and productivity have been destroyed. For example, those working in production industries might overlook the environmental impact assessment likely to be caused by industrialization in favor of production and profits. This in a long run may result in financial setbacks caused by degraded environment that can produce no more. This implies that the industrialization is not only a means to sustainable economic development, but also to a certain extent a means to destroying and degrading the environment when strict measures are not adhered to. Wherever development is taking place, analytical assessment must be carried out in terms of environmental as well as developmental sustainability. This should not disregard human, animal and plant life. Industrial residues have been known to affect all life around such industries because of their toxicity spreading all around.

Without compromise, development thrives well in a well-protected environment. The Christian practice is the source of commitment to fulfilling God's work and to realizing sustainable development. Let Christian industrialists not be among those threatening human, animal and plant life. Wherever Christians work, let them show that they are different from others. When Jesus told Peter, "upon this rock I will build my church, and the powers of hell will not conquer it" (Matt.16:18 NLT). There is a foundation already laid out on which developers should build and with that foundation, the power of corruption and selfishness should not tilt her position. The voice of the church in changing negative attitudes has been highly commended to transforming lost work values from economic to spiritual, but the unfortunate thing is that the church has also bent her voice towards other voices. The effort an industry puts in producing a piece of work should be equivalent or more to the required capacity to sustain the environment around it. To realize development, our work requires our physical strength, our mental capacities and above all, our spirituality; a complete development for a complete world.

God has placed us here on earth so that as we work, we worship him in Spirit and truth. Through work, we fellowship with God (Ps.95:6-7). That is the effort we need for reasonable development. Some people's efforts and interests are in making money, names, and destroying others. That is a fault caused by the fall and it will always crumble down our developmental work. Adam did not want to admit his own failure instead, he wanted to destroy his wife and avoid blame. To avoid such anomaly, Christians must accept responsibility where they work. It is not spiritually convincing Christians to work within a crumbled world of work and remain without being shattered or crumbled themselves. This may not necessarily apply to Christians only, but to all people involved in developmental work. How possible is it that the development of God's creation can be realized if Christians are crumbled themselves? There will always be need for spiritual effort in order to expect productivity and perfectness. Working among and alongside people without spiritual effort is a very rich mission field for Christians to exploit. That is where they need to take with them their spirituality[26], but cautiously that they may not in the end be absorbed in the system and quench the spirit of service in them.

Efforts towards environmental and sustainable development must go with commitment to the development strategies. However, there is another dimension of development and that is 'time'. Time is not redeemable once it is lost or mismanaged. When Paul advised the Ephesians to redeem time (Eph.5:16), he was not telling them to recover it but to guard against losing it, using every opportunity. Mackay an English missionary had also advised Christians not to be idle[27]. As they idle around and about, time keeps ticking and every tick to an idle person marks lost opportunity. The church must tell her members that it is not sustainable to lose what one cannot recover. Christians must learn from the Lord Jesus to engage developmental work wherever they might be and all the time, for Jesus told his listeners that he was working as well as his father was. People's response is to use the time given to them, which can be counted numerically but also in terms of productivity: quantity and quality. Time is a measurable aspect of sustainable development. Once it has been lost in useless work, space and time, even if the environment might be replenished, all other factors will have been undermined. Many people may spend time at their work places and fill the attendance book, but at the end of the day, they may not show anything equivalent to their presence. To be present at our workplaces

---

[26] Stevens and Alvin, p.1.

[27] Sophia Lyon Fahs, *Uganda's White Man of Work.* (New York: Young People's Missionary Movement, 1907) p.96

makes meaning only if we are engaged in developmental work. The parable of the talents in Matthew.25:14-30 teaches us how to invest our talents into sustainable development and productive work based on time spent. Productivity is not the only focus of development, but also quality; and quality is an essential measure of sustainability. A person who knows the truth about the importance of content should not ignore the role played by time and quality in development. The parable of the unproductive fig tree can also somehow explain the importance of commitment, effort and time (Luk.13:6-9). The Old Testament parable in Isaiah.5:1-6 of the vineyard that produced wild grapes can also explain how effort and quality work matters. Besides these parables carrying spiritual messages, they are also used from the outward to be true of what people do while they claim to be working and developing their environment. All the failures of productivity, quality, time and spiritual effort emanate from the 'fall'. In order to engage the world of work and development, the church must work differently from the rest of the other institutions, just as Jesus was telling his disciples that they should not be like the people of this world among them (Mk.10:43) which implies that there is a difference between church and other institutions. The fact that the world of work had fallen short of God's expectations we can never realize the expected development however much time and money we may invest unless we accept to invest spiritually and redeem the accursed earth together with our human failure, we cannot respond to God's creation and work mandate given to us at creation. Christians are redeemed to redeem others, work inclusive. Therefore; "We should see God's hand (in it) and be thankful for common grace as it operates in every friendship, every act of kindness, and every way in which it brings blessings to others"[28]; thus the horizontal aspect of work. The church needs to accept that she is an agent of development throughout her life in the marketplace. She is a missionary of theology of work and sustain-

---

[28] Wayne, p.665.

able development at home and away from home. In other words, the church must be development oriented before she can advocate for the same in the world out there. There is a lot of evidence that the church is a sleeping giant over a lot of land treasure, which has not been utilized for her economic empowerment, and yet she is lamentably poor. When she tries to be involved in development, she employs intermediaries who will use the environment for economic benefits other than environmental profitability, simply because the land developers who are using it, it is not theirs. The church on the other hand has not bothered to train her own members to specialize in the theology of development. To make matters worse, church property is collectively owned and as the saying goes; "what belongs to many belongs to none", the church ends mismanaging the environment and trying futile development through the hands of intermediaries and unskilled personnel.

12. Redemption of the Environment

Redemption is a measure of grace offered freely and serves to maintain the position of those who do not have the means to preserve their place in a community or save themselves from the power of sin. It follows a trait of inherent captivity and Grudem speaks of redemption in Christ as; "a progressive recovering of more of God's Image."[29] It is therefore evident that our redemption in Christ means that we can, even in this life, progressively grow into more and more likeness to God and be able to redeem the lost glorious environment; the home of all generations before, now and the years to come, by engaging in sustainable development. Of course with the population explosion, space is becoming competitive for urban development, industrialization, housing and wild life. Without doubt, the environment will be adversely affected and sometimes human beings will be at a disadvantage of being pushed

---

[29] Wayne, p.445.

farther into the nonproductive areas, and crammed up allowing no development of any reasonable sustainable measure.

Therefore, the biblical perspective of redemption connotes the divine intervention in the fallen world of humankind. The idea of redemption is a broad term but specifically it originates from the early Old Testament times when God redeemed his people like Cain with a mark from being killed (Gen. 4:15), Noah and his family from the floods (Gen.7), The Israelites from the Egyptian captivity (Ex.12), and it kept on being God's divine activity. It became the progressive development of Spiritual Grace. At the exit of Adam and Eve from Eden, God protected the Garden of Eden from corruption and developmental degeneration (Gen.3:24). All, including the "Eden work theology", they were put under protection. Christians are marked with the blood of Jesus Christ by Faith and should be able to become agents of development after their redemption by re-entering the Garden of Eden and resume work.

In the book of Revelation, God promises of a new heaven and earth. This implies that the original Eden which was put under protection from human corruption (Gen.3:24b) will be revealed and handed over to the redeemed humanity. That which must be redeemed must have been facing captive powers disabling freedom of development. Likewise, human work, which has been marred with undesirable patterns of bondage shielding it from the joy expected from it, would be redeemed too. Work in all its dimensions was intended to bring Joy, but the fall rendered it handicapped and ever since the fall, it has been associated with toil and sweat (Gen.3:17-19). The joys of work have been enclosed by the pain and toil cast over it at the fall. Evidence is so clear that when we sit to enjoy the benefits of our sweat, we often forget the pains and toil we had faced at the beginning. Despite God's declaration, many people would have wanted to skip the toil and sweat which would have resulted into more degenerated work ethics. The whole of human work pattern needs to be redeemed. Since the church are members of the redeemed of

God, she should not continue working in a world whose work patterns have purportedly remained fallen. She is the change agent who should redeem what was lost. When Jesus says, "You are the salt of the earth…you are the light of the world… Let your light so shine before men, that they may see your good works, and glorify your father which is in heaven" (Matt.5:13-16), he implies that the church should redeem those whose path is dark and who find bitterness and dissatisfaction in their work and work places; and illuminate their hearts and work place conditions and reduce the pain of those who are heavily burdened and who find it hard to realize reasonable development. If you are a manager or administrator, make sure your developmental plan is not theoretical but theological and not a chronology of events but a logical network. That will be one of the ways to maintain a sustainable but also a heavenly work pattern for development. We must avoid becoming a hitch and resentment to environmental and meaningful development just as Rehoboam did. (1Kings.12:1214). Listen to the good counsel in order to develop good working relationships. The curse that affected the workplace (Gen.3:17b-18), affected the human race (v.17c) and spread to the work itself (Gen.3:19), denying humankind to develop their mental capacities for reasonable development. The world of work having experienced multiple fractures needs to be fixed by redeeming and healing the very recipients of God's grace. Since redemption is a process of preparing for a better ending, then the redeemed and their work will finally enter into eternity. That is when the world of work will experience the 'rapture' long awaited. The end will have come, never to wait any longer. Salvation will then be made complete where humankind and the entire creation work will be liberated. Redemption process will have come to the full end where all creation and human work will be made new.

13. Consummation

When talking of consummation, the focus is on the good intentions of God's creation, which must find its perfection through the redemptive work of Jesus Christ; the final destination or goal[30]. Christians are the reflection of this intended completed work experienced in their everyday life. Therefore speaking of consummation, we are looking at the final victory over sin that has been responsible for the life's failures, and then look forward to the completeness or perfection of what must be leading to sustainable development. Part of the concern here is about the final act of God's perfection on our earthly activities. Everything will be made perfect as a bride prepared for the groom ready to consummate their marriage (Rev.19:7). Christians and their work will be presented before God with the record of all they have been doing (Matt.25:34b). Knowing very well the Christian focus of eternal life, we should guard ahead of time that our developmental work will not be found wanting. The development aimed at must be God pleasing. If you have been involved in aimless work, selfish work, degrading work, unsustainable work and unspiritual work, then know for sure that it will not be rewarded or credited. The biblical ethical dilemma presented in the book of Daniel 5:27 against King Belshazzar is one of judgments of what we do that are unsustainable in the sight of God. When the final day comes, every individual will give an account of his or her own work. It will be weighed and when found wanting, it will be destroyed. Human beings might have opportunity for reformation but not the work that will have become crooked. In his article; "God's Judgement Day", Oswald J. Smith says that we will be judged based on our attitudes[31]. Christian

---

[30] Consummation carries the idea of making complete as the goal of intention. In the case of work and development the focus is when these will meet God' final perfection for humankind.

[31] Oswald J. Smith, *God's Judgement Day (rev.)* (Belfast: Every Home Crusade, 1980) p.2.

workers' attitude towards development strategies are key to working differently from others, for they will stand a greater judgment more than other workers will, because to them God's standard has been revealed.

14. God is Rationally Relational Through Development Work

To be relational is to have a rational interactive and cordial working environment. God in his relational work makes humankind work like him. He wants work to be perfect and results oriented. He is not selfish like most of us do, for in his rationale he reveals his work plan. That is why at creation he made humankind in his likeness; giving them a home and qualities to work and behave like him. The church needs to keep God's character and work as a family in order to affect a rational development in the world where she lives and works.

God did not create a 'static' but 'dynamic' world of work with a theology and this made him an ardent worker and developer. Work is older than theology because theology came as a result of application of knowledge and utility of resources (Gen.1, 2; Jn.5:17; Rev.21:5). In his statement, "Let us make human beings in our image, to be like us. They will reign…" (Gen.1:26 NLT), God clearly shows himself that he engaged in the art of developing a working humanity and with the intention of working in fellowship. To realize development, we must avoid working alone but emulate God. Through creation, human kind was to have fellowship with God. If God preferred a lone working life, he would not have made a revelation of himself because he would have been all alone and 'self- contained'. His relationship design had to be manifested in his revealed work. For that matter, God appreciated what he created (Gen.1:31), portraying the spirit of a development worker. Human beings created in his image must bear the spirit of a 'Working and developmental God' surrounded by and with perfection. That is the absolute "Biblical theology of work". The very beginning of Genesis 1:1

tells us that the earth was formless and empty. When he finished creating, there was form and order and the earth was filled with his creation. God's creation removed the chaos of darkness and formlessness. Human work then should not reverse the world back to where it was before creation. Looking closely at what is happening today, the world is facing a new order of chaos where science and technology have been unwisely applied. The Christian who is one of the consumers of the products of science and technology must think beyond what he or she consumes, and be on a checkout of the future continuous and consistent production. This tells us that in the world of work where we are co-workers with God, whatever was disorganized by sin must come back to form and order, and the earth must not be left empty but must always be replenished for development and continuity. The curse pronounced on earth, has left it in the hands of corrupt human hands. However, those redeemed through the work of Jesus Christ can overcome it.

There is a lot of environmental unpredictability, it is more threatening in the name of urban and industrial development, and yet development without a theology is destructive and defying God's laws. From a Christian perspective, there is need to develop and teach an "environmental theology" otherwise humankinds stand to be wiped out of the face of the earth at their own hands in the name of development. Work and development must recognize the historical and theological factors of creation. As the hands work the earth, the head must direct the intentions and the heart listen to God to be able to control the whole of human activities. God well knowing that there was bound to be environmental degradation, He instructed man to replenish the earth. Today the theology of "replenishing" has been ignored in the name of development or it is not known and understood. As long as we engage our environment for various activities of developmental nature, whether as individuals or as corporates, we need that theology, and the church institution should be at the center of making it known. Real development cannot ignore the "theology of creation and replenishing", and this is not only in terms of physical development, but equally important in the spiritual and social development. There should be a theology of 'holistic development' accessible to us all, no matter the level of our engagement in development.

Therefore, looking back we see God as a rational and relational worker who worked with perfection, and put mechanisms in place to maintain his work (Gen.1:26b). When He says; "so that they may…" it gives the impression that human beings were created with the sole purpose of working as representative developers in administration or stewardship of God's estate. That is where all humans fall short. The church must know that she is delegated to do God's work among and through her members just in the same way God did it in and through Jesus Christ. The members may include among others; sweepers, security guards, drivers, teachers and preachers, bankers, doctors and even heads of states. The Biblical and Christian theologies of work do not spare any category of workers and type of godly work. Therefore the Biblical perspective is that humankind must work and work well wherever they are placed because they have the spirit of God, and the work pattern is heavenly (Ex.31:1ff), and revealed through Jesus Christ just as he declares: "All the father has shown me, I have revealed to you"(John.17:6). The church should work towards penetrating all developmental programs in order to help laying a theological foundation that would direct the intentions of the developers. As we engage work, the focus of development must not miss the element of the heavenly pattern of work here on earth.

Throughout the Bible, we have different images of God as a development worker, and these images help us to understand how each type of work is God's mission field through which Christians can manifest their development. Jesus portrays himself as a vineyard-dresser (John.15:1-8; Is.5:1-7). In addition, in this picture he makes us understand that in order the vine to become productive and sustain the owner, it must receive attention and conducive environment. The metaphor that Jesus used tells us that a conducive environment is necessary for a sustainable development and productivity; the two must go together. Although it might be a social, political, economic or spiritual environment depending on the nature of the marketplace, the need is so much pressing that, we must understand where we are coming from, where we are and where we are going.

The unique thing about Christians is that they must behave differently from others when they are working. They should see their work both vertically and horizontally. This makes work more divine and progressively eternal than being ordinary or momentary. According to Genesis.1:26-27; human beings are workers by make-up or design. They have the express command to work (Gen.1:28), which is repeated by Jesus Christ in the Great Commission saying, "Go…" (Mat.28:19). To all who are engaged in different types of work, the point is not only working, but also knowing that working is a command. Christians are called upon to work with their 'heads, hands and hearts' as the well-coordinated work in the likeness of God, *because in the hands lay actions, in the head lays visions and plans or ideas and in the heart lays the wisdom.* These make the likeness and image of God complete. However, many of us sometimes work with our hands separated from our heads and hearts or with heads from hands and hearts. For any sustainable development, the three must work together. (See figure 2 on page 31). The advantage Christians should enjoy against others is that they are able to understand the Biblical teaching that guides them on how to work with their hearts as well, meaning that their spirituality becomes a major component of their work and development goal.

15. Development as an Aspect of Stewardship

Development is a translation of what stewardship is meant to do, it mandates us to work and look after God's creation, and we know that in the process there must be marks of human activity that will influence the theology of sustainability. We cannot develop what is not progressively sustainable without knowing why we are here, who we are and what we are doing. Interestingly, the Bible comparatively is the most likely book that can provide the best resources for valuable and sustainable development for now and the ages to come.

The Biblical human work perspective is made clearer by painting it with a picture of God's mind or wisdom. This is what the Bible calls God's likeness. God had a purpose of sharing his likeness with humankind; for he wanted to assign them work, which they were to do, basing on the divine pattern and the expected development. People regardless of their backgrounds need an environmental stewardship developing out of their response to Scriptures and academic progression that can produce an environmental theology that can improve people's stewardship. Human response to environmental and developmental needs is a mandated duty. It is not an option. Our participation in environmental protection and sustainable development is our survival. We must not be careless and wasteful as we fulfill this charge. We are expected to take care of the environment as good stewards of development.

As we think of development, we must know that there are natural things that God put under our care, which must be replaced with new innovations or completely destroyed to pave way production industries. However, the question that must be asked is; what are the long-term benefits of the new project in relation to the environment going to be replaced or destroyed? The answer to the question must be well thought about because, as a good steward of God, we must make a critical analysis of what we want to do or not do. As had been seen earlier, road constructions tend to destroy a lot of natural environment. Swamps clean the water we use on addition to being a habitat for most of the aquatic life. Trees are good air cleaners absorbing carbon dioxide and a number of other pollutants, which would have otherwise poisoned the air we breathe. Green environment everywhere filter the sun raises from causing skin cancer. There are so many uses of the environment around us. We might want to save money by taking a short route to a successful project while we are leaving a very long negative impact on those coming after us. Therefore as good stewards, we need to consider many options in order to save life than saving money, for many does not make life but rather life makes money.

In Eastern parts of Uganda, Busitema had a very conducive habitat for Baboons, when people turned to the forests where they lived, they started to roam people's gardens, compounds and even houses, destroying food and threatening children as well as adults. To be good steward, we must consider all other animal and plant life around us so that we avoid causing environmental chaos. Whatever development we put in place must respect others to an extent of thinking of additions rather than subtractions.

IV

DEVELOPMENT
AS A THEOLOGY OF STEWARDSHIP

In the biblical account of creation, God gives humanity dominion over the natural world, to look after it and to use its resources as God intended. God gave mankind the ability to take care of his creation, a skill to manage, and through these skills God became visible and heard to be speaking to mankind as Genesis 2:15 tells us that God gave man two responsibilities: one was to dress the Garden, and two was to keep it. These two carry the ideas of physical working and spiritual care. This then gives development and stewardship as a theology of work, for when we work as was directed by God, we become God's stewards and good managers according to his likeness. Stewardship is both more of a spiritual and physical virtue of service to God than management, which is more of physical and social engagement, based on acquired skills. This has always provided the Christian justification for material progress when they manage well their resources but becomes negative when the spiritual virtue of stewardship degenerates and the focus of generating wealth becomes the top agenda. However, with recognition of our role as stewards of God's creation rather than our own, we become better mangers. This then, sounds to us that to be good stewards, we become good managers too. As a church, we have a particular responsibility to the environment and concerns of sustainable development. This is more evident now that there is continued growth of the rich people threatens existence of life around them globally as we know it through global warming and other environmental changes.[32] The search for wealth and status tends to overlook the sustainability of our environment and stability of life, and without doubt sooner or later wealth generation will reduce and eventually stop when human life degrades and dissolves like ice under heat, because there will no longer be conducive environment to support it. Every Christian worker must guard against engaging in unsustainable development, because any neglect whether intentional or unintentional, it will affect life negatively and will be a matter of judgment. In this respect the church acts as a steward of God's resources through her ministry no matter where, and will be answerable to what has happened under her care no matter the circumstances prevailing at the time. The wisdom passed on to us and the skills we acquire are all meant to support what we do in our developmental work. We cannot continue in the name of development when seeing the environment depleted of its capacity to sustain life. The church institution as earlier said is a good or better vehicle, basing on the Bible teaching to tell the truth about human responsibilities over creation. Her theology is live and dynamic that no matter what religion one is, the Bible remains an authoritative "Book" that speaks out to all humankind about their responsibilities over creation as God's stewards.

---

[32] Rich people are mostly behind environmental degradation. They put up mega projects that tend to overlook human needs by looking at their need more important. This in turn raises questions about whether God will forgive us for the damage caused upon the people and the rest of the environment unnecessarily, and whether He will allow humanity and the earth to be destroyed by human action in this way.

16. The Voice of the Church and her Role in Sustainable Development

The church is God's voice and therefore must declare his intentions for humanity and all creation. Wherever the church exists, it must be of one mind or purpose, one voice and of truth. She should step out critically and defend her mandate as God's voice without allowing unethical, immoral and corrupt practices against her assigned responsibilities. Therefore, she should speak one voice otherwise; things will fall out of her control. Recently, the Anglican Church from a socio-spiritual point of view spoke differently on matters regarding sexual deviation behaviors and it caused a rift among the leaders and the believers. If the church knows the truth and her responsibilities, her role is to be effectively involved in whatever is being done or not done for the good of her mission and the work entrusted to her here on earth. The God the church serves is universally one, and therefore she cannot speak or act differently. The Church's engagements are crucial and necessary in directing sustainable development for humanity's sake, no matter where on earth.

For example in the abolition of slave trade in the 19th century, human trade was encouraged in Europe and America but it was not sustainable because it many African countries lost a large population in the process of capturing and selling locals. Africa lost work force and even future brains. British Christian politicians and evangelical scholars decided to present their case in the British Parliament (1759-1833), and people like William Wilberforce, delivered rousing speeches on the floor of the House of Commons, galvanizing public support for the abolition. Although Slave trade was a very lucrative business to individuals and nations, it was not a sustainable business from a humanitarian point of view. When Christians raised concern like Wilberforce and William Granville who served as Prime Minister of the United Kingdom from 1806 to 1807, Slave trade gradually lost support and died out. This kind of testimony tells us that the church and the Christians have a big influence in any political, social or economic agenda.

In that case, considering the issue of development, the church is not excused from engaging in sustainable goals because it is for the good of everybody in the interest of the creator. That is why in the market you will not only find products from a single producer but instead from different people, sharing different products and skills. When people exchange such products and wisdom, the have not's get services they would not have otherwise received and amazingly their joy becomes God's glory. That is what sustainability aims at doing, and it will always bring the Joy of our work. We should never restrain ourselves from doing our best for our environment as we engage in development because it will bring happiness and joy to God's people, while God is glorified. If we did not know, this brings sustained relationships and continuous blessings.

17. The Joy of Developmental Work

Development in many ways is redemptive because it puts in place services that are badly needed by the people. It redeems people from social, physical, economic and spiritual needs. In fact, development that is pro-people helps them to be spiritually alert and brings joy to whole humanity. Therefore, work was and is meant to be a human joy by engaging in it like God, engaging in it into useful development that will last even for those coming after us. People who work every day know how fulfilling it is when they look back and see the marks of what they have been doing, especially when they win the approval of others. However, caution must be made to find out who the people appreciating their work are. Their work might have been corrupted physically and spiritually with and by the people around them and they turn out to be the ones appraising their work. People, who really get down to enjoying the fruits of their toil and sweat, know very well how their hearts are always soothed with and bathed in joy. All good and satisfying things are meant to give us joy. If God was delighted with his work, surely without doubt there must be joy when we are doing it and producing results he expects of us. In Genesis.2:15, God to Adam depicting work commands two words. One is *abad* (work), and the other is *shamar* (take care). These words can also be used to mean "service to God" and "keeping of his commandments" which correspondingly would mean stewardship and development. It can literally be translated to mean, "Work for taking care of". Nevertheless, in a broader sense, service may mean development in relation to the field of ones work. For that matter work is a service of enjoyment and development, but also a command from God. It is therefore the church's primary role to make development as an important work agenda both in her pastoral and evangelism programs.

The concept of secular and sacred picture painted against work has created a worldly dichotomy that tends to overlook the fact that service and development work for the good of God's people has no boundaries. As long as that work has religious values, it will remain sacred. Whether you are a medical worker or carpenter, sweeper or tax collector, if that work is done with honesty and in humility, it will reflect a sustainable spirituality of work, developing into people loving themselves and their work. If development becomes destructive, then it is not sustainable. Anything that destroys people's joy, and instead brings pain and misery, it is not developmental and sustainable (Gen.3:17-19).

Today there is a lot of suffering caused by climatic changes all over the world emanating from the misuse of our environment in the name of development. Whatever we do that aims at gratifying our desires and personal joys, it becomes the sorrows of others, and loses its spirituality. It only keeps rotating around self with no vertical or horizontal focus or orientation. Work should always be understood as service of development, and development as a product of God's work which then becomes sacred. Work was never intended to be secularized because God the author of all work was, is and will never be secular. God remains God and as such; divine or sacred. His nature never changes, so are his works. The church should take it upon herself as a spiritual institution to disciple her members on how to become good developmental workers for sustainable development. She should remind her members that their work and workplaces are the points at which they meet and fellowship with God (Gen.3:8; Lev.26:12; Deut.23:14). However, she should also note that when she does not do God's developmental work and do her own, she behaves like the untrusted steward. She should be a steward in order to steward people to become good stewards of God. Whenever church leaders stand before God's people, they must speak out the truth about God's agenda for humanity. The truth about Adam and Eve hiding as a cover up, or Cain against his brother Abel are indicators of work failure to develop a communion or fellowship with God, because they had separated their hearts from God's work. When we become discon-nected and not sure, of ourselves, we distort the work agenda that was designed for us. Many people hide in their personal work failures dis-guising as if they were fulfilling God's work. When they are discovered or things go wrong, they push the blame to others. Yes, others might have contributed to the failure, but it is very healthy and Christian to admit our personal failures before we look at the failures of others. The church has been on the African continent for more than eighteen centu-ries[33] and surely, it has done a great deal of preaching, and providing social services like hospitals and schools, but has failed to sustain those developments. In spiritual matters, she has a problem of making follow up programs. Some schools however much they are founded on Chris-tian principles; they are driven by the economic pressure more than

---

[33] Christianity first arrived in North Africa, in the 1st or early 2nd century AD. The Christian communities in North Africa were among the earliest in the world. Legend has it that Mark, one of the four evangelists, brought Christianity from Jerusalem to Alexandria on the Egyptian coast in 60 AD.

spiritual value. The focus of development is motivated by generating money more than generating a God fearing generation that will serve God and the nation. Some governments are now beginning to control religious institutions with stringent rules and as a result, these institutions have started to lose their moral focus because many of the lawmakers do not have the heart of God, but rather are looking for what can benefit their egos. That kind of direction is and will never be sustainable. It has already resulted into rolling out graduates who are inclined to making the world devoid of God's touch, for they have lost the faith-based values because of the National policies and laws tending to overlook the contributions made by the church and people's spirituality. A number of Church founded Health facilities are not performing well. In other words the Church in general started good developmental work but has not been able to sustain it, and one of the many reasons for her failure is that she relies on the donor funding or small funds from her poor congregation, and yet she is one of the major land owners the world over. Confucius as quoted by Miller says; "Choose a job you love, and you will never have to work a day in your life."[34] Meaning that when you love the work God has assigned to you, you end up never knowing that you are really working, because the love of your work overshadows its challenges and the human unmet expectations. We talk of the church collectively, but in sincerity, some of us, her members and leaders, are frustrating her collective developmental goals. Most of what the church has failed to sustain, was left by Colonial Missionaries and Masters more than five decades ago. The development registered thereafter is more of retrogressive than progressive work. Church members are no longer interested because their personal joys have not been achieved. In this case, the church becomes what she is because of what her members and leadership is able to do. If the leaders understand the Scriptures and

---

[34] Miller, p.14.

contextualize its message, there is no doubt that valuable and sustainable development will be visible.

18. The Sacredness and Secularism of Sustainable Development

The sacredness of our work is entrenched in its eternal destiny, knowing that once it has been started, it continues as a service to God. As God lives forever, our work must have values that will never diminish. God knew what we were and are capable of doing here on earth. He prescribed a heavenly pattern, because work came from heaven down to earth through God's word. Therefore, God works in and through us and our work must remain visible as a sign of his presence. Work tells history of God's presence in the life of his people and entire creation. When one looks at the great Egyptian cities of Rameses and Pithom, "the two store cities the Israelites were forced to build for the Pharaoh of the oppression",[35] they become evident of the great works. Although they tell us of the suffering of the Israelites, yet we see that the great hand of God was at work embedded in the suffering of his people; the Israelites. Developmental work comes at a cost but has rewards. You will understand that the construction of those two cities by the Israelites under Egyptian slavery was for their own good. Firstly, in disguise they got plenty to eat which could not have been possible if they had remained in Canaan. Secondly, they were able to multiply greatly in order to make a nation. While the Egyptians were interested in their building projects, God was interested in building a people of difference. We may sometimes concentrate our minds on the suffering we are likely to face at work or the limited benefits thereafter, and we try to avoid them by undermining the sustainability protocols.

---

[35] J. D. Douglas et al, *Article on Rameses in the Bible Dictionary* by Carl E. Devries (Grand Rapids, Michigan: Zondervan, 1987), p.845.

No matter what people go through as they work towards sustainable development, the church has the responsibility to make them understand that development is not a walk through or a mere talk but a very serious engagement towards sustainability. Aware of the fact that what we go through as we work towards sustainable development may not necessarily be for our direct benefits, the church must be responsible for making people committed to working both in good and bad times and their work should remain visible for the good of all. The sacredness of our work is the concrete attachment to, and the relationship it has with God no matter the circumstances we face, because at the end such work must leave positive impact as a witness to its sacred focus.

The secular idea may not be erased from our minds because of what we have inherited and goes on around our work and us. There is a tendency that most of us workers do not live with our God given hearts at our workplaces, instead we live with Satan hardened hearts denying us to control our working behaviors. People see work as if they own it and therefore they will do it as they wish. Differing from the Greek dichotomy of work into sacred and secular, I see work taking its secularism in the Garden of Eden when Adam took control of himself to determine what to do. Whatever we do outside Divine ordering becomes secular. To such people, there is nothing like accountability. Secularism has no feeling of and about God. It is merely human pleasure or displeasure. It is a worldview set against a sacred worldview; each of them with different ethical values, where the sacred worldview has both the vertical and horizontal outlook more than the secular, which has selfish outlook with little focus on either of the above outlooks. Therefore, secularism becomes a practice where most of the people are working for their personal goals with no interest to serve God and his creation. With secularism, everything runs under human control influenced by Satanic forces, and does not take in mind the outcome of what is being done or not done for the interest of others because it has the characteristics of declining influence of religion and diminishing religious beliefs and diminishing authority[36]. People displace others and other creation for their personal indulgence and are happy when they are doing it without thinking about how sustainable their actions are for themselves and others. It is at this point that the church must come in and provide better alternative measures to ensure that there is a sustainable co-existence and interdependence when thinking in the direction of development. Secular mentality divorces God completely from all human engagements. Any development that does not take in account God as the author of creation, is not sustainable. The role of the church here becomes crucial by speaking out for God's creation in the world of diminishing spiritual values.

The idea of sacred and secular work which was borrowed from the Greeks has therefore continued to give misleading beliefs and practices that work which has no ordained calling or spiritual connection is ordinary work and therefore secular and that which was holy or connected with God was sacred. For that matter people's concepts have changed the face of the earth because of the way they think and work. This then seems to imply that what is regarded as secular work is completely sanctioned and completely controlled by man. As longer as we look at what most of us do as secular, we shall continue to mess up with the most important developmental work intended for our productivity and sustainability. However, we must know that apart from Satan distorting the focus of work and its values, work remains God's work and what the church has to do is to refocus or redirect it heavenward more than keeping focused earthward. In that case, one would think of might be the priestly work, which was and has always been regarded holy calling. Of course, it is true to say that before the fall of man, all work was holy until human disobedience corrupted and degraded it. From that point of view, the Greeks saw all human efforts as worldly especially if they

---

[36] Wesley Carr, *The New Dictionary of Pastoral Studies* (Great Britain, SPCK, 2002), p.326.

were inclined to self-satisfaction. Going back to the Garden of Eden, Adam was supposed to do manual work according to the term "dress" (Gen.2:15). This tells us that within that work, everything of human life was inclusive; spiritual, social, economic and political. God did not separate these dimensions of human work because God himself is not divided. Whichever area of life we find ourselves working in, it is God's calling and it is holy. The problems that have been caused by dichotomizing work into sacred and secular domains, has led to resigning our minds from thinking holistically, and as a result we have degraded it to only serve our personal desires not knowing that it was eternally designed to serve God for the rest of our life from one generation to another. So looking closely at this assigned work at creation, it was sacred work and not priestly or clerical as we understand it today.

19. Accountability

Whether sacred or secular, we are accountable of what we do or not do. All work intended for developing the environment was assigned for every human being. God needs that accountability at some point in one's life. We should not be contented with collective responsibilities before we take our individual responsibilities. We are endowed with different talents to do different roles, but all contributing equally to the same creation. People should not hide behind a collective name like; 'the government' or 'the church' thinking they will get away with their mess. A single person's mess can spoil the whole lot. Therefore, as humanity, when we engage any type of development here on earth, we should note that we are doing it as God's stewards, and we must observe the rules of the game. However, according to the Greeks, people who worked, as clerics were the only ones looked at as doing sacred work. That concept led Aristotle a Greek philosopher to deem work as ordinary and to be tinted with corruption and therefore not befitting to be sacred. Looking at that kind of reasoning, people who degrade work values that are not related to priestly or clerical role, do not see themselves as having done anything wrong because to them it is not part of sacred work. The Greek people in the ordinary business led the early church to be distanced from engaging in it, suspecting it to spoil the good intentions of the church because of its human tendencies to corruption. The position of work became more critically tilted towards its failure than its success. This kind of reasoning has influenced the attitudes of many Christian leaders and workers that their responses towards developmental work, has never realized the desired sustainability. It led many people to doing work their own way for it did not portray an accountability element to anyone superior. Therefore, today when we are looking at the role to be played by the church in sustainable development, we are revealing a failure of so many centuries back in church history. The subdued voice and engagement from a secular point of view if not dealt with pragmatically, the church, as an institution will never have a positive role to play locally and globally in sustainable development. That may lead us to thinking that this might be the reason why most of the developers can never associate God's presence in their work, because if they do, their work will require a standard that they be guided by Christian ethical business values or principles. We must know and appreciate that work will remain with us, but also be aware that the Greek Hellenistic tendencies will keep nagging around, and therefore we must be cautious of the implication of what we do or not do. Based on the Greek philosophy, development has declined because it has overlooked its sacredness and regarded secular and individualistic tendencies. The heavenly focus has been lost. However, we cannot deny the fact that all good work is God's work and therefore sacred. We must allow our development attitudes to be heavenly driven in order to meet sustainability and accountability. In most cases, our developmental minds are inclined to our human desires to see ourselves successful men and women by keeping our names remembered. But we need to be aware that although man does not live forever, the positive or negative impact of his/her work will remain to tell the story, where this story will be told as history, in form of an account of the origin and progress…the knowledge of past events…[37]. The story of the Tower of Babel is one of the examples of development that was intended to pronounce and promote human acclaim above God's glory. For they said, "come, let's build a great city for ourselves with a tower that reaches the sky. This will make us famous and keep us from being scattered all over the world."(Gen.11:4). Whenever you read that story, it should remind you of the futility of our efforts in development when God is not involved (Ps.127:1-2). It is then very clear that there are many developers, who want to keep their names remembered more than the importance of their work, and yet it stands as a violation of God's divine order.

However, it is important to note that the command to work was given before the fall and hence it is meant to be part of the development work done and the sacred engagement rather than being ordinary or secular. Today many people have not come to terms with developmental work because of the hardships involved before realizing its benefits. Despite the hardship and toil, it should be noted that work had been liberated as Jesus declares; "Look, I am making everything new." (Rev.21:5) This newness includes the accursed work. People whom Jesus has liberated, have a liberated mind to liberate the endangered environment as a habitat for God's creation. Jesus redemptive work liberates humankind, their environment and the accursed work. This demands that the church comes out to pronounce her position based of the Gospel of Christ that transforms humankind and the environment around them. Holistic development is therefore possible and a likely reality, not in future but beginning with us right now. The toil and conversely, the idolatrous work, are all the result of the fall, and the new-

---

[37] A. M. Macdonald and E. M. Kirkpatrick (Eds.), *Chambers Everyday Paperback Dictionary* (Edinburgh: W & R Chambers Ltd, 1977), p.338.

ness is the result of the Cross developing from the work of Jesus Christ. The real suspicion with which most Christians see vocations in any marketplaces is caused by the drive to selfish ambitions or greed for wealth and power or other sinful motives like it was at the Tower of Babel, where instead of developing a lasting relationship in their work with God, they separated themselves because of arrogance (Gen.11:4). Unfortunately, the world today is not willing to integrate the theology of spirituality with her work because when it comes to giving accountability, the cost is very high for the ethical standard demanded. The influence of greed and wealth in politics and leadership has overshadowed the truth as portrayed in (2 Kings.8:18). Church leaders who live their spirituality at the altar, and Christians who engage in politics and leave their spirituality in the pews in the church tend to bend easily to earthly desires and forget the essence of their calling and their work in development. It is very possible to make all business including politics sacred by engaging the creation mandate (Gen.1:26). If it is as true as Paul claims in Romans 13 that all leadership comes from God, it makes leadership sacred and Christians engaged in political leadership can guide their subjects towards sacred work, thus sustainable development.

20. Redemptive Developmental Strategies and their Cosmic Scope

Despite the impact of sin that has left scars almost everywhere, redemption has brought about healing no matter the greater and deeper visible scars. The entire created order has been redeemed through Jesus Christ. When Paul talks of God reconciling everything in Jesus (Col.1:20), it includes even the accursed hard labor that receives liberation through the redeemed humankind. The phrase "All things" includes all realms of human engagement be it physical, spiritual, social, political, mental or otherwise. It can therefore be concluded by saying that the process of redemption that started at the Cross, whatever God created awaits the final day when the process will be complete and all will be set free from bondage as Paul again says in (Rom.8:19). The universal extent of God's redemption means that everything affected by sin and the curse, including the ground (Gen.3:17) and human work (v.17c), will be redeemed. Holistic development will be a reality and Jesus Christ is the vehicle of God's redemption through his Church by the power of the Holy Spirit. If there is any institution on earth that can realize total development; it is the Church and Christians are the true agents of this development. Christians are supposed to portray God's presence (Matt.5:16-17), and show Godly development values (Prov.16:11; Matt.5:13-16; Prov.20:10). A Christian ought not to live a double standard life while at work and workplace. Just as James asks, "Does a spring of water bubble out with both fresh water and bitter water?" (James.3:11) That is why to be "salt and light" are required of every Christian to lead others to seeing and serving God with their work. Christians working with the mind of God should not allow unethical, immoral and exploitative tendencies in the name of development either to the environment or their fellow workers. Biblical and Christian theologies make up theology of work and comparatively are more development oriented and value focused than most of other theologies. Whereas development is important and necessary, the way it is intended should avoid detrimental impact to both human beings and the rest of the creation. The developed countries have for example found it easy to advance their development programs while making the developing countries the dumping grounds of their residual and degraded materials. This has also translated into what the developing countries are doing when they are paving way for some developmental projects they make some poor people's land dumping sites for garbage.

There is a lot to learn from Jesus holistic ministry. From heaven, he came with powers to perform a kingdom ministry to show God's presence and care for his people. Jesus did not only meet the people's physical needs but also took care of their emotional, psychological and spiritual needs. The diverse gifting and opportunities of the Church can now be justified by the multi-faceted nature of God's mission, fulfilled in what the church does and can do. The scope of the Church's progressive work in the redemption process should extend beyond the Christian communities as Jesus talked about the love of a neighbor using the story of the Good Samaritan (Lk.10:25ff). In this parable, Jesus showed how the Christian ministry could develop beyond our human set boundaries. The scope is very broad and limitless.

21. Development as an Indicator of Restored Work

The characteristics of restored work are embedded in visible development. Jesus in his teaching used a number of parables in which work and development were central. He used a parable of the fig tree that was not producing fruit, which partly was not developing into a useful tree. We know Jesus used this parable for spiritual purposes, but allow us to literally use it this way that the owner of the garden had wanted it cut down for it was wasting space (Luk.13:6). It might not only have been wasting space but also time invested in its care, including the anxious waiting of its fruits. This helps us to note that non-developmental work destroys many expectations, degrades values and wastes time. When we do not yield fruit from our work, we cause multiple wastage to ourselves and others supposed to benefit from our work. The church is an instrument that God uses to bring to reality what work must produce. The Church should work for restoration of what the world has lost. Any work that is not fruitful is non- developmental. Jesus himself was born in a working family and community, where he engaged in his parents' work. When he started his ministry, the central theme was "work" focusing both on the spiritual and physical realms; for he called his first followers to work as fishers of men, a call from physical fishing to spiritual fishing. He from time to time tried to develop the mental capacities of his followers to understand their calling as change agents in the world of work. This included both the physical and spiritual capacities to develop their God given environment.

The Church therefore has no way she can separate work from development or vice vasa and continue to claim to be the true institution of Christ. Paul Stevens and Alvin Ung assert that Christians are called to develop the potential of creation and to make human imprint here on earth[38]. Since Christians are the members of the church they must endeavor to meet that obligation. For that matter, Christians are used as reference to development, and we must note that they are not developing a Christian world outside the ordinary, and not even doing it alone, but they are developing a Christian worldview of work based on the Biblical teaching and they can be only referred to as an example within a context. All people are called and equipped by God, to make sure that there is something positive they are doing. Development is a footmark of mandated human work and it is a witnessing activity of involvement and productivity. The church is likened to the human body of many parts with different functions for the common good of the whole. When we want to realize development, we must work together as a body or family. The woodworker, the brick maker, the stonecutter, the roof maker, all work together to producing the best of a long lasting house. If one of the workers does not do the best of his or her work, then it will have a negative effect overall, however much of the best work others might have done it.

22. Foreign Economic Dependence

The church works within a community of different working institutions, which might not be quite aware of their God serving abilities and their mandate as God's workers. Aware that the church has one of the

---

[38] Stevens and Ung, p. 3.

largest membership among other religious institutions here on earth of 2.2 billion members, the equivalent of 31% of 6.9 billion world population[39], it is surprising that she has been undermined and denied the opportunity to influence work and development issues because of the superior economic powers and strong corrupt tendencies supported by political selfish leaders. Small as the church might appear to be in some given localities, she can use her great position as the springboard of influence to all of the human race in developing the world around them as she speaks for God authoritatively especially over her members. However, for the church to succeed in influencing the direction of global sustainable development, she must equip her leadership well enough to be in position to address issues relevantly and adequately. Every church leader, no matter the level of education, must grasp the importance of speaking to Christians and non-Christians around them the importance of focusing on sustainable development. The church leadership cannot stick on the salvation of human soul and risk the silence on the perishing environment, thinking that her future is safe. It is unfortunate that one of the challenges the church faces to play her role efficiently and convincingly, is her inability to generate financial resources from her vastly owned land, especially as it is here in Uganda. A case in point, is her land which was donated to her by the late Ham Mukasa at Ntawo in Mokono district, which was estimated at 640 acres, but now has greatly reduced because of squatters who took advantage of no development taking place on it for almost ten decades[40]. Without shame, the same church having failed to use her land resource has instead continued to depend on donations from abroad. That kind of dependence cannot sus-

---

[39] Information accessed from www.pewforum.org of 2010, on October 12, 2018

[40] The land is situated in Mukomo Municipal Council North of Uganda Christian University, which currently has the ownership after the Province of the Church of Uganda gave it out to support the development of the University. However, development of the land had failed because of many squatters who have made personal developments on it causing conflicts and court cases.

tain the church for long, because of two things, which have already been noted here as, 1. During the western economic crunch of 2000 most of the third world countries that relied heavily on outside funding had a very big drop in development and other infrastructural projects. 2. When most of the churches in Africa (especially Church of Uganda) broke ties with some of the Western churches the financial support were withdrawn. Because of the felt financial deficit, some church leaders decided to keep their ties alive in order to keep the financial flow running and protected, while undermining her spiritual life. They quietly went ahead to solicit for financial aid to support their long started programs. This kind of behavior, points out to us that the church's economic dependence was and is not sustainable, unless she embarks on utilizing her vast land resource she owns. Although we are talking of the "church" as a unit, the blame will always go to her leaders. When they fail to strategize the utilization of the available resources and guiding the Christians towards meaningful use of such resources, they will always turn to seeking aid outside their churches, missing the developmental focus the church is supposed to advocate for, and maintain for her members for today and tomorrow. Therefore, having failed to develop her own institution sustainably, she has lost the voice to advocate for the same among other institutions, especially the government, the umbrella institution.

23. Sustainable Development

Development is a long-range dimension that puts in perspective what the future should be like or would want things to be through combined efforts. What has been said above is not a reference to all churches in the world. There are good examples of the church work emanating from her members' work that can challenge other Christians in the world how to work in the same spirit. One of them is John Cadbury who started to make Cocoa and drinking chocolate in 1831 in Birmingham. He was a Christian of the Quaker denomination, which was formerly known as the religious society of friends of the 17th century in Lancashire[41]. If we calculate from then to today and how the company has continued to produce the products without undermining its original quality and goal, then we would know that once Christians set their minds towards a developmental project, driven by their spirituality, that project for sure would stand the test time. That was what many people would have regarded as secular work because it was not priestly, but it has served people for the good cause for generations. Another person is Henry Ford, an American captain of industry and business magnate who founded the Ford Company in 1903 in Dearborn, Michigan USA[42]. Although he was not an ardent believer, he was raised an Episcopalian. At least we are made to believe that the Christian faith and values affected his behavior and career that he left behind such values that have determined the credible product of his Company to the present. Another category of the great Quaker Christians who started one of the outstanding institutions in the world were John Freame and Thomas Gould who started Barclays Bank named after James Barclays; the son-in-law of John Freame in 1736 on Lombard street in London. This Bank has been in existence for the last 282 years[43]. These three examples shade light on the contribution the Christian discipline and church can make in development of any kind. In which case, Christians should not stand aloof or isolate themselves from the plight of much needed sustainable development in a world of almost diminishing resources. We know that because of lack of understanding and interpreting Scriptures, most Christians have inherited a wrong perception of work to the extent that any work with gains is related to corruption. The point is that development can only be registered where there is physical progress, and when we look around, most of the progressive work has some kind of relation-

---

[41] https://en.wikipedia.org/wiki/Cadbury (accessed 08/08/2018)

[42] https://hollowverse.com/henry-ford/ (accessed 08/08/2018)

[43] www.historyhouse.co.uk; http://www.banking.barclaysus.com/our-history

ship with corruption which is not a sustainable development trend. For that matter the church has left her responsibility to other individuals who have destructive development intentions.

In the Anglican Church of Uganda, there are many examples of failed projects because the development agencies did not put in place sustainable development measures, or they did not know their work, or they corrupted the system to the extent that it failed to yield any acceptable results.

24. Judgment on our Development.

At the culmination of God's salvation purpose when Jesus will come again, all institutions, all religions including Christianity, will be judged for their work, their faithfulness as stewards with the resources and responsibilities entrusted to them by God. Even those who have never read the Bible will have no excuse because God in his wisdom has communicated to all humanity their mandate as stewards of his creation. However, the Bible is very resourceful to helping Christians and none Christians to know much more that they have material resources, gifts, training and skills (Mt.25:31-36) to develop themselves and the world around them. The judgment criterion puts into perspective God's expectations of every one, but especially Christians, because God's expectations from them is higher, broader and deeper, and it validates their present human work in all their different capacities. It must be clear that if the path of the wicked leads to destruction (Ps.1:6b) then the works of wickedness have no future, while the works of the righteous and faithful will be truly rewarded (Rev.2:10b). Does the church feel challenged by this Scripture, knowing that as an institution, she must perform works that will attract reward. Looking through the Scripture it tells us very plainly that unless the church takes upon herself the roles assigned to her as a voice to the world, the reality of sustainable development will not be realized favorably in the interests of all. Caution however should be sounded to her leaders that it is their responsibility to guide her members and the rest of the world to that goal. People may have the will to do so, but leadership slow to move towards that will. The Scriptures are very clear saying that: "My people are destroyed for lack of knowledge: because you have rejected knowledge…" (Hosea 4:6, KJAV). The church appoints leaders for the sake of leading the followers to the truth. Followers will lead others, in their communities who are non-Christians, just as Matthew says in chapter 5:16, that the believers are the light that shines upon others to show their good works, so that they may in turn give glory to God who is in heaven. The church's response to sustainable development is reciprocated in people giving glory to God. In a world where people are lamenting because of unfavorable social and economic environment, however much spiritual they will be, will always drag them to worldly unfulfilled desires and eventually suffocate their love for their God. That is one of the major areas the church must deal with., The church must bring light to the people in developing their different capacities, that in the end they will show their active participation, to be able to influence their families, communities and nations.

Whereas God gave us the mandate to utilize the creation around us, he created in us the spirit of discernment and freedom of choice. What we choose to do or not do may mean a lot for us and others for today and tomorrow, although it might not necessarily be in equal measures, and not immediate. If the benefits of what comes out of what we choose to do or not do prove to be sustainable then our Christian worth or character will have proved its authentic acclaim as being heavenly. Therefore, without doubt, the church's role is of a primary value in the Global sustainable development. The diversionary measures taken in the name of development are misapprehensions of what God's nature of work is and therefore will not be defended on the Day of Judgment. As long as environmentally our development becomes abusive and unsustainable then we have no excuse because the Bible provides the best resources for teaching and rebuking those taking the wrong direction.

25. Work that Lasts: in the New Heaven and New Earth

The reason we need to talk about work that lasts is that when we talk of sustainable development, it must be with a long lasting impact. Work is eternal because it is of God and by God. Work began with God, and ends with God. It has no end. No generation that comes and goes with work. Therefore, when we engage in the development of God's resources, we must be aware that development must stand the taste of time, measured by its physical and spiritual lasting marks. It must be inscribed on our hearts and the face of the earth. Some generations come to the world of work and sometimes leave nothing of their work behind and to the worst, they destroy what they found there, but God's work remains and lives forever because he had inscribed it on the face of the earth to testify for all generations. How then can it remain on the face of the earth and not in our hearts? For example, cities have been built and destroyed, roads built and abandoned, bridges constructed and broken down, but God's works of creation have remained over ages and will continue to exist until that time when he will make the new heavens and new earth, removing the corruption that destroyed its beauty. Christians' spiritual final destination will be glorified material, a destination described as a new heaven and a new earth (Rev.21-22; Is.65). The new heaven and new earth will be dwelt in by the redeemed people and their redeemed work in their new resurrected and glorified bodies (1Cor 15; Phil.3:21; 2 Cor.5:17b), and Jesus declares that he has made all things new! (Rev.21:5). The Revelation of John declares that; "… all nations will bring their glory and honor into the city" (Rev.21:26). "The bringing" can be both material and spiritual presentation that will last forever: including our love, kindness, and faithfulness, our skills and impartiality to God's work. These revelations strongly suggest that there will be continuity with the present but which will undergo dramatic and cathartic renewal (development). Revelation 14:13 assures Christians that in the new heaven and new earth, they will rest from their hard work. This does not imply doing nothing, but engaging in the original work that did not demand toil.

V

CHURCH'S COMMITMENT

Commitment is not an idea. It is a paradigm shift in action, which destroys all the former neglect, laziness or idleness and careless work. The church's commitment comes as a sacrifice because it defies other ordinary demands, which might stand in her way as she works towards better goals. When we became members of the church, we became committed more than ever before because we accepted to follow a new order that is more of listening and doing than it were before we were redeemed and converted. While non- believers are more committed to doing damage; the church teaches her members to be more committed to mending and restoring the lost values. When we become committed, Jesus assumes more power and authority in us and controls our activities and without doubt, he shows us the way. What destroyed our relationship with God is ever around and determined to destroy our developmental goals. The church has the responsibility of tuning her members to a more listening and doing position like the master worker when he speaks out, than idling and engaging empty talk.

The church is supposed to be a change agent in the world. She is not only meant to deal with the anticipated spiritual world, but also with the physical and social world where she lives. The focus should be on how to use the bible to appeal to the physical world and then theologically to understand its contribution to the understanding of work and development and its concepts in different marketplaces. Jesus' command "Go into the world…and make disciples" (Mk.16:15) is a marching order to go to work in different marketplaces and make disciples of both spiritual and physical develop in and of our environment, and this marching order was given to his followers, whose responsibility was over "the entire world". The church therefore has been mandated to subdue all negative forces contrary to well- intended development goals and is supposed to bring the whole world to the awareness of God's work, no matter the challenges she faces, she must take charge of what people do in relation to the redemptive work of Jesus Christ. Unless the church engages the world of work, her mission to sustain development and protect the environment will only and just be apparent or detrimental.

26. Challenges Faced by the Church in Maintaining Sustainable Development

As we all take on work, we must focus on developing our minds first so that what we intend to do can have meaning and impact on those we intend our work to serve today and tomorrow. Anything that defies work values will automatically destroy its fundamental objectives. The church should have a critical eye as development is being carried out, but the question is; how can the church overcome or avoid external and internal challenges that can destroy development when most of the developers and political leaders are not supportive of the church's concerns.

It is also important that the church must identify the kind of challenges her members often meet at their work places that affect the output of her work and undermining her developmental choices. However, one of the major challenges undermining God's work is caused by listening to ourselves more than listening to God. When we listen to ourselves, we do what our hearts desire, and when we listen to God we do what he desires us to do. That is an inner inability that intercepts God's communication to us that others may not be able to see. That brings to us the hitch of "selfishness" which cannot allow us to hear God speaking or see the needs of others. Our work and services begin pointing to "self". The truth will be that we are really working, but also another truth will be that we are working only for ourselves. That kind of work has no intrinsic or extrinsic values, because it does not develop beyond self. The idea of sustainability connotes extended service beyond self and the present. The role of the church and her members is to stop those who work for themselves and by themselves. When they die, they leave nothing behind because the good ideas and goals they had for their development are buried with them. In this case, what the church should advance to all developers irrespective of their creeds is that work ideas and goals must be shared, and evaluated or assessed before development takes place. No one owns work and therefore work ideas are God given for the benefits of others, and the development thereof is for the good of all. Unleash the ideas and you will enjoy the benefits of your work with others while still living. God in his loving care disclosed his work pattern and plans to us so that we can also disclose them to those around and those coming after us.

There are challenges the church cannot deal with because of lack of political authority. For example when political governance has no will to listen to the plight of the church, no matter what the gravity of the matter may be, the church will stop at that and no more. Another serious force that the church cannot overcome is the economic venture. Most of the development being done always is under the government policies and not church policies. As it progresses, the natural environment becomes the victim of development. Because the biggest focus of the government is the economic development more than any other development. Some of such issues raise little concern because the power behind it is influenced by selfishness and corruption. Should any concern be raised, some corrupt people will give them a blind eye as if nothing has happened or will happen. What can the church do when she has no authority to intervene by stopping such developments? I am not talking as an anti- development. No! Nevertheless, as one seeking the position of the church when development seem to be taking a negative direction. The church is a red flag raiser where problems are likely to occur so that the policy makers and implementers can critically analyze the situation before things become worse.

Today, spiritual matters are taken more lightly where economic and political matters are the overriding factors in the public eye. Whatever the church's concern is all about, it will appear as if she is denying the beneficiaries of development their intended goal. Whether the church's voice or intervention is constantly heard or not, development of any nature will continue to thrive, supported by selfish leaders.

Challenges were not created to hinder our progressive work but rather were acquired from the deceiver who in the process of advising human beings becoming knowledgeable they became stupid and foolish by trying to own up, thus missing the step towards their success. Knowledge indeed was acquired but it became the knowledge of destruction instead of construction. That is why the idea of Christian reconstruction is very relevant in order to reconstruct the old and ideal theology of work in the Garden of Eden. In Mc Vicar's examination of Rushdoony's Reconstructionism, he contends that Christian Reconstruction has contributed significantly to how certain forms of religiosity have become central, and now familiar, aspects of an often-controversial conservative revolution...[44] This tells us that in order development to make sense, certain forms of religiosity must apply especially those that find their roots in the Biblical theology. Unless the church takes her right position in the development of the environment, those still here longer, will witness the dwindling resources as the human population grows. There will be need for food and shelter, which are the most demanding human needs. Space will no longer be available to produce enough or to build more houses because already unsustainably, we have destroyed the environment in the name of development and when real

---

[44] Michael J. McVicar, *Christian Reconstruction,* accessed on www.thegospel coalition.org published 2015

need for development comes, there will be nowhere and nothing to develop. This will more than ever before affect the population growth and people will die of hunger and disease because of poor housing. I am not blowing a trumpet, because I said those who will be here longer. The evidence is very clear because of global warming, desertification caused by deforestation, over grazing, over population and irresponsible industrialization. As we move farther into new era of science and technology, the impact of what our present environmental usage demands will pull down all developmental ideas and progress.

One of the church's primary calling is to have fellowship with God. There is no fellowship without a common identity. Our calling demands that what we do should reflect what we believe and live for. Our work and workplaces have hitches that interfere with developmental goals, our joy and happiness. Some of the hitches are character generated while others naturally come by the nature of the environment of our work and work places. However, our work becomes developmental when we love it and do it with all our efforts right from inside our hearts. The heart is the center of most of the controversies and therefore it determines most of our work practices and behaviors. If our mental and spiritual capacities are incapable of discernment of the ideal sustainable development, then our environment will not hold the future generations. Not many of us realize the most things that hold up our development from sustaining our needs. We rarely sit and think about why our work is not making good progress or why we are held up and we sometimes end up even destroying the works of those who are keen at making impressive results through what they do or not do. Whether we belong to the church or not, we are all guided by the spirit of the creator through what we believe as part of the "moral ethics", but because of the evil one, at more than any single moment, we find our souls sapped up and un able to do the best even alongside those who work ardently. There are glitches and drawbacks along our work journey. Many times, we are not concerned and passionate about the productivity of others. All that mater is what we think we are worth, no matter the quality. We are good at draining up other workers' efforts, sometimes not aware that we are digging ditches on the same road we are travelling, because work is not an individual venture but rather cooperate. When we undermine others' work in any way, we are like someone dribbling his teammate or shooting in own goal.

Glitches and drawbacks are very common in most of our work places including palaces, state houses and even in churches. In 1Kings.22:6-25; two prophets did not agree with each other because one wanted to water down the credibility of the other in order to win favor from the king. When some of us want favors, we tell lies, we promote envy, jealousy, enmity, greed, pride, and many others. These may not appear direct detrimental developmental glitches but they are brain generated and heart driven to the extent that when they surface in form of works, they become so destructive and repulsive to the acceptable ethical and moral standards. This kind of scenario is not sustainable because eventually it will bounce back and destroy our personal intentions. This ends in chaos or crises among workers and workplaces. It does not matter who you are or what your nature of work is and where it is, the reality shows that, no workplace where work hitches are not experienced. However, there is a possibility that such hitches or drawbacks can be overcome no matter how deep rooted they may be.

In this book, we find a number of issues discussed concerning hitches or call them "Soul sappers" among workers whether in private or public workplaces and the way how they destroy industries of all types, leaving the proprietors rootless and hanging, sometimes finding it had to overcome them once they have crept in. They have become responsible for undermining sustainable development especially in the developing countries, but not forgetting that the developed countries have more often been responsible for the failures of the developing nations. The heart of a worker must needless be like the heart of a destroyer. Christians must build one another because the benefits of their work are collaborative and distributed equally. One, who destroys another, is destroying oneself indirectly. God at creation made each one of us a capable worker with potentials to be like others and work like him. The devil however became a serious virus and caused humanity to 'sin' and everything became a mess. The work and the worker were both affected. The only anti- virus known to improve our work behaviors is "repenting" which can renew the imperfect work values and improve workplaces. You want to be good at work and make your work good; the turning point is renewal through Jesus Christ. It is biblical and true to affirm this truth because realities show that serious Christians produce perfect work. Someone out there might not be a Christian but working on the same principles of Christian faith, and the sensitivity of his or her work becomes felt among God's people in a positive manner. People of different faith and political or social divide fill the market place, and to have their productivity felt and appreciated, there must be a change of heart and thinking. The work moral ethic must focus on that which is value based and God edifying. Less than that, the ditches and hitches will continue to broaden and deepen; challenging workers, producers and consumers.

27. The Problems Facing the Church in Mitigating Sustainable Development

Besides physical hitches to sustainable development, other spiritual hitches undermine church work, resulting into unsustainable development, and social instability, and we cannot exhaust all of them in this book. However, we shall try as much as possible to address some of those hitches that are commonly experienced in our development work and workplaces either coming from within us or from our co-workers, regardless of our status levels. Although such hitches are in most cases unstoppable, there are spiritual resources available to enable the church overcome them as Stevens and Ung propose in their book; *Taking your Soul to Work* (2009). If you ever wanted to prove yourself unworthy of God's expectations in your developmental work as a church, try to rely on the decisions of proud people especially leaders and you will see how the hitch of Pride will destroy all your good work. Other hitches like Greed, Lust, Anger, Slothfulness, Envy, Restlessness, Boredom, and Grumbling, Rumor mongering, Lies, Selfishness, Stealing and Criticism are common in the church work, and they greatly affect well-intended development. Therefore, once we are under the influence of any of the above, know that our work has no future, instead it is being eaten up slowly and eventually it will be no more. Such behaviors and practices do not sustain development unless we accept to be guided by the spiritual resources available for us as a church so that we can be helped to overcome those hitches and hold ups that interfere with our work output or productivity, whether they are physical or spiritual. Most of the church work has been completely submerged in a number of hold ups and sometimes without any one helping to discover what could bring about renewed work both spiritually and physically. God in the book of Prophet Hosea 4:6; was against the death of his people Israel in ignorance because of their leaders failure to guide them. When you see a persistent fault at work and workplace, know for sure that the leader is either involved or absent or ignorant. The involvement or non- involvement of the church, her absence or silence in presence, and possibly her ignorance of what is being done has got a big impact on the social, political, economic and mostly spiritual life of the people. We know and believe that the church is the voice of God with no restriction. Therefore, speaking about sustainable development is part of her mission. However, admittedly most church leaders do not understand what their role in development is or to what extent they should be involved. They therefore cannot approach developmental issues when they are ignorant or less informed. This would demand that for the church to claim her divine mandate in directing development, she must have her leaders well equipped with information, knowledge and skills. Paul in his letter to Romans... says, "How will they hear if they are not told? (Rom.10:14) The church has to be concerned about the social and physical wellbeing of her people using the pulpit. Is the church aware that salvation is holistic in nature, to liberate human beings spiritually and physically? If so, to what extent has she influenced her congregations, and if not so, what must be done for her to be involved and direct her members into sustainable development?

Most of the time the church's mission has been aimed at spiritual development on the expense of all other human needs and this has resulted into suffocating the joy or happiness of her members' work. Christians have sought for happiness from the work they love to do, but seldom have they found that happiness. Many people find happiness not when they are working but when they are either eating or drinking and mostly spending the money paid for their work. Did you know that during the month most of us work under hard conditions without enjoying the work itself, but that at the end of the month when we get paid, no matter whether there was any development made or not, we go out smiling and enjoying what the money can do for us. The people must enjoy development, right from where its engines begin to rotate. It is at the engines of production that sustainability begins to determine the direction of development. Whether manual or mechanical, we should begin to love our work. If only it makes meaning for all of us. However, the question would then be, is it sustainable for all? Some of the church traditions we find at work places deny people the opportunities to work heartily and happily[45]. When we try, the traditions we find at the work places become more pronounced than what the Biblical teaching is all about

---

[45] See the Greek mentality by Aristotle

There are things that come our way without knowing from where they come, but there are also those, which are inherent in us that interfere with our work, and without question, we know them. Sometimes, we try to work on them in order to keep good working relationships in case they are causing rifts at work. Sometimes, we do not know how we behave at work. We never see ourselves as problem causers at our workplaces, and even to other fellow workers. The outcome suffocates the values of others and the ethical justification of why we must work. That is where the church as an institution of both spiritual and social change must come in and take its prophetic role to make a call to the people especially her members who can be easily accessible and tell them how sustainable development is their creation mandate no matter the challenges they encounter. Some of the hitches that affect sustainable development are situational and in most cases generated by selfish ambitions of some individuals especially leaders. Some of the few examples commonly affecting the church's role in mitigating sustainable development are discussed here below.

28. Pride: The Proud Leader

How does pride affect sustainable development? First it is both a spiritual and social vice; a show off, or feeling that one is important and self-reliant even when making decisions of public interest. Pride brings someone to a point of seeing oneself as overall, where decisions are made by one person as the only brain above all others that is capable of directing the important decisions. The person looks at self as one with better brains than others in the public sight. Carr calls it; "arrogant desire to be superior to others… one of the seven mortal sins and is often considered the supreme vice. It is anti-social."[46] Since development is for

---

[46] Wesley Carr (Ed.), *The New Dictionary of Pastoral Studies,* (Grand Rapids, Michigan: William Eerdmans Publishing Company, 2002) p.281

social benefits, Carr rightly describes pride as anti-social. Okholm also calls it "the inordinate desire to excel over others and God, often with malicious intent."[47] Whenever it stands in the way of realistic developmental programs or projects influenced by personal ego, know for sure that there is that great sin behind an individual or a group of individuals called pride. Pride quenches the spirit of hearing and listening, appreciation of other people's contributions and continues to suffocate good intentions. Okholm in fact went ahead and said that pride is the supreme vice against humanity. Thomas Aquinas had explained in Latin that pride is superbia, which is related to covetousness. There are people who in the name of development covet the property of others ending up displacing them or causing social violence with a feeling of pride of; "what can they do to me?" Any kind of development carried out in that way defies human dignity and cannot be regarded sustainable as longer as it violates the rights of others. This cannot be called sustainable development even if it might be in the interest of many and can earn the government a lot of revenue. The few will always end up in a complete social dilemma that will affect their economic and spiritual wellbeing. The responsibility of the church is to first of all condemn the spirit of pride, then help developers to think in terms of balanced development which does not disorganize human stability in their places of habitation no matter how few or many they may be. Development is well known for its public gains but also for its majority or minority deficit. However, there is good pride and bad pride. Good pride is that one that recognizes the contributions and successes of others. It recognizes ones success for the benefits of others without marginalizing them no matter how much or less they have done or will do and contribute. Good pride is that one that sees others at the same apex and capable of even being better performers. They can contribute developmental ideas for the good of all

---

[47] D. L. Okholm, in his article on "Pride", in the *New Dictionary of Christian Ethics & Pastoral Theology.* 1995, pp.685-86.

without taking advantage of and over others. Church leaders, who see themselves at the top of decision making, and their work as all abiding, should never distort development plans from others in case they themselves do not have anything to contribute. The growth and development of the church is the seed growing in her members and not in her leaders. That is why the church has structures, like Synod, Council, Boards and Committees, through which developmental plans are passed, in order to avoid decisions made by arrogant leaders and developers. Unfortunately, in the political leadership, the spirit of pride is greater than that one in the church, and this creates opportunities to give proud leaders openings for corruption. To have sustainable development plans, there must be sustainable structures, which must play their roles so that the future has a sustainable foundation. In some churches, some leaders assume too many responsibilities in determining the future of the church and they forget that their position in that church is temporary as compared to that assumed by members of the mentioned structures. When such a behavior creeps in the church leadership, the same church cannot have a positive role in determining the future of any sustainable development. It is therefore important that a church leader, of all things must shun pride because it destroys reputation, credibility, focus and programs. If pride over comes a leader, the leader tries to undermine good ideas and destroys development resources. The quality of a leader is not measured on an all- round knowledge, but on a just representation of all other capable members. After all, the leadership position is always one at any given level. Therefore, a leader is one among leaders with whom he shares views or ideas for sustaining developmental plans and projects. A leader that is convinced of others contributions cannot be ashamed of saying; "I am proud of you", or "I am proud of our achievements." That is good pride because it is not demeaning any one in any way. On the other hand, a leader who is self -possessed with bad pride causes negative attitudes against others' contributions and their work. Such a leader may not be ashamed to point out that; "Had it not been my efforts..." In this case, such a leader does not sustain others' ideas and achievements. He is not supportive but instead he pulls down good ideas and works in order to promote his own achievements whether they are good and acceptable or not. He is a captive of pride. John in his first letter, chapter two verse sixteen says; "For the world offers only a craving for physical pleasure, a craving for everything we see, and pride in our achievements and possessions. These are not from the Father, but are from this world". As long as our pride is for self-gratification, whatever comes out of it will not sustain our work.

One of the most important things to note here is how the church can overcome the challenges brought about by pride in our work and at workplaces in order to sustain well-focused development, since pride is blind to see reality. Pride builds on shaky ideas and shaky grounds that eventually it will be challenged in the context of sustainability. We may not be of the same mind because not every worker is spirit filled and influenced, but the truth will always remain that Christian moral ethics are very central in transforming work behaviors especially when engaging in public as well as private developmental work.

Sustainability has many faces. It can be economic, social, physical or spiritual. Whichever the case might be, we cannot disassociate one from the others because Christian work is holistic in nature; and the church's mission is to effectively address herself to local and global concerns since she is a family. She can therefore address herself to the whole person and the environment thereof. That is why we find it fundamentally objective to speak of the church's role to be of primary importance when discussing both the local and global sustainable development.

We can therefore expose pride from a negative point of view, where it is regarded as a hindrance to development and assumes beyond what is not, looking down others contributions without ever looking around one-self that others can do or have done something worth or more important than theirs. Sometimes the fools or ignorant pronounce them-selves more than who they are or what they are supposed to be. It is not until they and their works are rejected almost everywhere and they begin to ask what the problem was. When they are told the truth, they never even accept that that is how they are behaving. They will instead turn around and devise all possible means to destroy what is already working for the good of others. One developer was reported of illegally buying off people from their rightfully owned land, arrogantly saying that they were poor with no security. When justice could not give back their land, the developer turned around, and offered the same people jobs on his farm. He saw himself as having now become their salvation because initially he saw them as poor people and now he was giving them work to do. Was that a justifiable development plan? Was it sustainable? Did you know that the proud assume that their proposals or projects can never fail? They know everything and can do everything. They are the advisors, and without them, nothing can work. They talk all the time because they think they are knowledgeable, and they never make mis-takes. To the best of their expectations, they occupy the best of the seats at the high tables of decision-making, and without them, they know nothing can work. They are the people with the best brains and words. They carry the day and expect to become the talk of the occasion. If your public agenda omits them, you become enemies. Oh! What great fools. The proud are the best fools for they never know when calamity is about to befall them for all is well with them. Happy moments to them have no end. They can even walk on hot charcoal bare footed thinking that their wisdom is good enough to survive them the heat. The reality will always tell if they are wise. God says; "I will not tolerate people who slander their neighbors. I will not endure conceit and pride" (Ps.101.5). This tells us that pride is not a virtue of sustainable develop-ment.

At our work places, proud people are dangerous because they will not allow or accept anything to be true or perfect if it has not come from them. Any development program that has not involved them is not sustainable. The story of Sanballat and Tobiah is evident of this pride and arrogance (Neh. 4). Does the church know such people? If so, what is her action? They will overlook all contributions and plans unless they have a contribution in them. At every occasion, they think that their input should be sought and when given, they must be respected. They think if they are not consulted, things will misfire. All success comes from them for they are the brainworkers. Unfortunately, when things go wrong, they are quick to jump out and attribute all failures to the rest because for them they never fail or make mistakes. The proud think they have open eyes of seeing others as proud but have blind eyes to seeing themselves as a folly. If you have never noticed it, most of us have different levels of pride but to some extent, it might not be as dangerous as to overlook or undermine the work of others. As it had been said at the beginning, don't be surprised that even among kings in palaces, heads of states in state houses and priests in churches, you will find this hitch of pride there. One may wonder why a King or priest should be proud. Nevertheless, remember they are human beings. They have that inherent sin. Seeing themselves at the helm of the entire population alone can make them proud and sometimes think of themselves super human or as small gods. In this case, they are the motion movers and all development work is from their mouth. If you want to discover why some of the African leaders are hard and stubborn at relinquishing power, it is all pride; "I am who I am, what can they do to me? I know it all, who can do better than me?" In the book of Isaiah chapter 14, a proud and arrogant King of Babylon is portrayed and his disgraceful fall. Yes, Pride breeds prejudice and later a fall. Unfortunately, when the proud fall they do not fall alone, they destroy all the development done during their tenure and they damage many institutional establishments to which they were attached as supervisors. They destroy their families' integrity and they leave behind nothing of their best because everything will be associated with their pride. This tells us that whether we agree upon or not, developmental work must be disassociated from pride if it has to realize sustainability be it social, religious, economic or political. Pride falls with its structures and new era is ushered in regardless of its ability to provide a better alternative or not. There will be nothing taken from its internal value. Our human judgment, usually looks at the external, which in most cases, kills the good within us. If there was anything people can avoid; pride should have been on top of the list. It kills beauty, intellect, our mental capacities, nations, culture and important beliefs. It destroys people's constitutional rights, destroys riches and status, and above all, it destroys our spirituality. Proud people can never articulate issues based on public interests because they are always arrogant and self-centered. They do not see, feel for or hear others.

Pride is deadly because it kills personality values and imports impersonation. When we begin to lose ourselves to external motifs, that is when people begin to see our real selves, because the virus of pride begins to manifest in our words and actions, especially when things begin to go wrong at our own hands, and we begin to jump out, pushing responsibilities of failure to others. If the development program is rejected or fails, our withdrawal will drag many out of the system, convincing them that what they are doing is impossible or is likely to hit a snag.

When pride enters our development plans, many faults and failures begin to affect our responsibilities, especially in the church, where nobody is willing to take responsibility. Church leader tends to push the blame to the Christians and vice versa, the hitch created will go beyond remedy, and whether we like it or not, the problem will grow more and more because nobody is ready to own it, simply because one person assumed too much. The skillful will withdraw from expressing their views because if they do, the proud will interfere and claim their contributions and when things fail to work out the proud will try as much as possible to avoid becoming a public "sorry" for what has happened. There will be a lot of time spent in arguments about who is responsible for the mistakes or failures and what appeared to be an individual problem would end up affecting others, and work for some time will be at a standstill; there will be no productivity. Pride will result into; loss of self-esteem for individuals, relationships, productivity in the production industries, loss of income in the economic market, loss of social interactions, and to a large extent, it will affect the religious or spiritual moral value of work. We need to think out ways and means of how the church can overcome the problem of pride eating away people's personalities and their work values affecting their relationship with God. In most African countries where leadership has been tagged to tribalism, when the proud leaders fall, they fall with many of their tribes' men and the future of a nation or church becomes dark.

There are Biblical examples and other present-day examples that we can reflect upon in order to help us understand how deadly pride can destroy our character and our works before we are completely wiped out of sight. Biblically Saul was a great king of Israel who was as well a good fighter. His pride lifted him higher to the extent of seeking for the life of a young and inexperienced fighter David, only to be ashamed when David showed him his spear and a cut from his garments, which were to point out that although he had guards around him, David was better guarded and had better opportunity over him. (1 Sam.24:1-11; 26:5-11). Pride under develop our thinking capacities because it can breed hatred and a sense of superiority. Pride can blind our eyes, close our hearts from understanding God's plan for the people we work with, and why they are working with us. We see ourselves as the only traditionally accepted and capable performers not knowing that our time sometimes has run out and other people must come in with new development plans, which can be sustained for a longer period than what we have. However, because our eyes and hearts are not responding to situations around us, we ignorantly and forcefully hold onto plans whose time has long run out. We must understand that development makes meaning within a given span of time, but can outlive that time if it had a long-range focus. The Biblical dimensions of development beginning from the time of creation are specific in telling us that the abilities given to us should help us to sustain the universe through what we can do or not do. If anyone was to be proud, let him or her be proud in God the superior sustainer of all creation, and avoid using ones position to jeopardize God's developmental plan and enviously chase after others because of their good developmental plans. Listen to this short narrative and understand how we can each be an amazing wonder in God's work.

We went to a building construction, which was coming to its completion. From the outside, the roofing showed a lot of intelligent architectural design. The walls from outside showed a builder who took his time to take every care in putting up bricks one on top of the other; full bricks, half bricks and even quarter bricks were wonderfully put together in amazing patterns. We found the window glass designer who was amazing to watch; for him he never climbed a ladder to go up and measure every detail of the glass size required. Instead, he stood in front of the window, which he wanted to fix, help up the glass sheet in front of the window and after that brief imaginary measurements, he placed it on the table from where he cut the glass and after he would climb the ladders and fix the pane. What an amazing talent! As we moved in, many people were at their different assignments; the plumbers, the welders, the floor tiles' fixers, electric cable wiring, painting and many other odd jobs. It was so amazing that what each one of them was doing fitted in what others were doing. Whomever we talked to was like feeling happy with self but also with others because there was that feeling that if others were not there his own work would not make sense. That was good pride in what others were doing. That is what we can call sustainable work or development because each ones work was an integral part of the other and it was not a stand-alone piece of work. However, we cannot avoid noting that there are others, who will never be proud of their own, and not even of others' work. Instead, they will try their best to put damage in what has already been done by their fellow workers. They feel that their friends should be discredited while for them they will be credited with good names. In the narrative above, we can see that the building when completed would have many hands on it but with a common beauty, for God had put his mind to work through those people.

Goliath was a man of immense strength and experience at war who arrogantly overlooked David as a mere boy; "sneering in contempt at this ruddy-faced boy" (1Sam.17:42), thought he was nothing before him, before God he was a wonderful warrior, and Goliath's contempt brought himself down on a mere stone thrown from David's sling. (1Sam.17:32-49). Human strength is given to serve God and not to fight God's people. If ones arrogance is to overlook the strength of others, then whatever comes out of their labors will be the fruits of arrogance with no spiritual value. We must learn from this story that size, age and experience are not the determinant of acceptance and success. Developmental ideas and skills do not come from strength, seniority or experience, not even from money and social or political status. They come from whoever God chooses to use, but most of all those who listen to his voice; the church. Therefore, the church must endeavor to prepare people of integrity who can sustain development. It is not true that strong and heavily build people are always successful, especially when they are working contrary to their God given development mandate. We always look at young people as incapable of delivering or performing where the older ones have failed as it was the case with David's brothers and Goliath. When we allow God to use the church in the local and global development planning, we become protective of what he assigned us as his stewards.

Don Moen sang: "*When we walk with the Lord in the light of his word, what a glory he sheds on our way, while we do his good will he abides with us.*" This is a very clear indication that unless we walk with the Lord, our development strategies might become impossible to achieve. Doing God's will abides in what we do. Any development that does not reflect God's involvement is not sustainable. The church has the role to bring to the understanding of all people regardless of their faith that sustainable development is walking with the Lord. This brings us to another important fundamental idea that unless ones heart is with the Lord, all developmental plans that may be thought out might end up in jeopardy. At our work places, we must guard against pride because of what we think we know and have against what others have or do not have. God occupies the positions and the chairs we occupy though us. The day God takes them away, we become powerless and useless, only to find ourselves at the mercy of those we thought weak and useless. We must appreciate the contributions of others whether great or small as long as they have a role in development. The church has to develop the spiritual capacities of all people besides their mental and physical abilities. The heart and the brains are more at work than the hands when we are working for sustainability. Pride is a spiritual deficiency of effective and sustainable development. The church must overcome it.

In the Book of Isaiah chapter 14, we read the story of a Babylonian arrogant King, who in the process of conquering other nations and killing their kings never saw himself one day being conquered and even dying. Nevertheless, when he died, the story clearly tells us that he was even rejected among the dead. The story is good enough to tell each one of us that in the world where we are living; is a place of our work for the glory of God but also it is a place of our folly. We do not elevate ourselves and think that we can sustain ourselves there. Unless God stands with us, we cannot boast of anything to our credit. In that case any development that defies God's voice cannot be sustained a while longer.

The Lord in Jeremiah says, "Don't let the wise boast in their wisdom, or the powerful boast in their power, or the rich boast in their riches. But those who wish to boast should in this alone: that they truly know me and understand that I am the Lord who... brings justice and righteousness to the earth" (Jer.9:23-24). Even if God makes us great, let us not make our greatness a source of power for tormenting others to the point of destroying their lives, their work and the love for their God. God determines our fate. Pride is the seat of destruction but a stepping-stone for redeeming and elevating the marginalized. We have many people among us who are behaving like the Babylonian king. We never have eyes to see the road end of our lives. The only thing we are able to see is undisturbed road of success where we are working and walking. All our work seem to suggest that we are here to stay no matter what others have put in place before us or what they will after us. Ours is the best and the road is always straight all through. The only disturbance we can see is positive; and that is from one level to another level, higher and higher. While we eagerly want to excel with our work, we are not aware that in the public eye we are falling from one level to another and that what we call development is in fact a sustained retrogressive journey to destruction. Pride's best joy is the downfall of others people's work and their personal character, while for them they climb up. There is a saying that what goes up one time will come down. Therefore, we need to be aware that we can never stay at the top. Our assumed good work cannot be sustained not until it has passed through the furnace of humility and integrity. More often than not, when proud leaders fall, they fall with their work and this suggests that their working strategies were not sustainable. Nature is an equalizer although it may not be in the same proportions. St. Paul advised that he who is standing should be careful that he does not fall (2 Corinthians 10:12).

Whereas it is true to believe that the church has done her best to fight against pride through preaching and in counseling, it has to be pointed out that she has also been sapped up in the same web and cannot any longer be able to speak out authoritatively against such a vice. The spiritual development that once was thriving among developed nations to greater heights has now died down and some of those nations are only known for their immoral vices, their destructive developments like the development of nuclear weapons and atomic bombs, psychological and biological wars. Not every step they take whether social, political or spiritual carries sense of value any longer. Leaders have come out to support anti human bills and actions, and many of them at the end of their term of office have been implicated of embezzling public funds, entering bizarre agreements that cost their countries exorbitant pay back, in the name of public and institutional development. They leave their countries in debits and dire need for transformational and fundamental leadership, not only in civil and political services but also in the church. To know that the church has been swallowed up in pride, some leaders do not listen to what Christians say or propose to hem, instead their word if final or decisive. In that case the church leaders cannot take a move to offer any critical advice in developmental plans.

29. Political and Power Influences

Today most of the church leadership in many countries has involved itself in political systems of the day missing the purpose of her mission in the world, even when it knows that it is doing wrong things, which are not sustainable, because the moment the system collapses, the church leadership will also collapse. For the church to have a voice in sustainable development, she should avoid being partisan in order to have a neutral position of advisory role. In Uganda, there have been systems of governance at different periods. It is well known that church leaders who had identified themselves directly with some of them, when those systems collapsed, their leadership came into critical balance. When they were still in support and were supported by such systems, they felt they were at the top of the ladder and would not listen to pragmatic advice. Pride of association lifted them up and left them there hanging when the new system came in. What we are sharing here is that to be developmental, it must be for the good of the people. That is why the church is the right institution to speak of sustainable development, for she cannot be compromised by powers around her. She represents everybody regardless. Some religious leaders have supported systems even when they know that they are developing their countries upside down.

Sometimes, church leadership has been accused of failure to understand the political atmosphere and instead have become victims of purported poverty in the church. When political leadership finds the gaps in the church, it swings in, pretending to fill the financial deficit, while it is seeking manipulation of voters. Some of the donations given, are neither geared towards the required development nor are they sustainable. Donations such as vehicles are good but expensive for the church to maintain. The church would have done better if she bought vehicles she can manage and maintain with her means. The church assumes that such a practice is in good faith, but in most cases and particular circumstances, that gesture carries a hidden political influence to the weaker members, who see it as a good will from the government. This is a common practice in Uganda, at least for the last twenty years. It is for sure not sustainable because as said earlier when another system comes in power, the donations will cease and the church will more seriously begin to feel the setbacks. In other words, the practice is not sustainable. It even denies Christians to do their part for critical development because they will always see the political leadership extending its hand to do what they should have done. This is similar to churches that heavily rely on foreign donations. It is not yet accepted by many that the offer is not sustainable, because it has been said that some few leaders who seem to support the systems, receive the cars and donations, they feel privileged and part of the high ranking and honored people. It even puffs them because they are seen treated like privileged 'others'. It might not be a wrong prediction that soon or later, the government might begin to pay salaries of religious leaders if these institutions do not come out to support themselves through their local and ordinary means. When such a decision takes place, the church will cease to preach the Gospel. She will muddled up, and the truth suffocated. The point to note here is that when the church receives state offers in the name of support, she will begin to withdraw from her primary roles of carrying out fundamental development among her members and the nation as a whole. She will not even speak against unjust development programs because her voice will have been muzzled up with gifts and donations through the leaders. We must remember that the beneficiaries of government donations are individual leaders not every member of the church. When they live in comfort, they forget their primary role and they begin to speak arrogantly seeing nobody other than themselves at the top.

Something you might have heard said that, "where there is a Bishop, there is the church" and possibly the Muslims might also be saying that where there is a Khadi, there is Islam or Mosque. That is not theological and not even biblical or Quran based. It is emptiness and vanity. It is not spiritually sustainable. If it were true, the church would have died with their leaders when they die. Instead, when some of them go or die, the church becomes even stronger than ever before. This implies that, the statement is not true, but is simply concocted by power-seeking church leaders. We must know, and it is biblical that the church is the body of Christ. The church is, because of Christ and not of bishops, while the bishops are because of the church. Act.8 provides information about the development of the church and the methods used to sustain it. It was a church without a bishop. Development is not an individual venture but a cooperate business. The church exists because of two important factors: the first is that Jesus Christ is the founder, and the second one is that

Christians are her members. The bishop is just a member of this church. Therefore, if the church is to be recognized for her role in sustainable development, she should move away from individualistic mentality or sentiments, and take collective ideas, participation and responsibility. Move away from politicizing its leadership power, move in for sustainable development. Most leaders seek for what the world can give more than what heaven can give. I say it with boldness but also with humility. If we wanted to assess any kind of sustainable development realized by the church without doubt, we would find it where leaders work with their church members as a unit. You will bear with me that most of the failures have been caused by church leaders; selling church land, failing to protect church property, misusing church funds and what else; mismanaging the flock of Christ to the extent that some of the church leaders have been chased out of their churches disgracefully.

If it were true that where there is a Bishop, there is a church, then at the exit of such a leader, the church would also make an end. Surprisingly when they go the church, sometimes this time becomes stronger than before. Remember the church has been called the body of Christ not the body of Apostles or Bishops with the intention of bringing his light into the world. The church therefore works as a body to bring development coming from her heart and then to the world; the kind of development that will serve God, his people and the rest of his creation for ages to come. Unless the church recognizes its primary role in sustainable development as a body, anything based on an individual member be it a leader or otherwise that will not recognize the voice and contribution of others is not sustainable. As a body, when one church member or leader goes, the others continue working together and even using the good ideas left behind. A church that listens to one person is dead except if it is Christ. Even if one is mighty in spirit and body but disregards others, soon or later there will be a failure in developmental schemes.

Pride of physical strength destroyed the mighty Samson, a man whom God had blessed with strength and wisdom to destroy Israel's enemies, but used it unwisely to flirt with women more over from the enemy side. His power and strength gave him pride to think that he would always get over his enemies as he had always done to them. It is not always that our human wisdom and strength hold on forever, especially if we use them wrongly. Any development done without recognizing God's voice will stand for a while and disappear like mist. Some of our contemporary leaders seem to appear as if they were beyond any threat of down fall or even death; leaders like Amin of Uganda, Gadhafi of Libya, Sani Abacha of Nigeria, General Bokelo of Central African Republic, and even among the incumbent leaders there are those who think they are indispensable in everything. Bragging is a symptom of deep-seated pride. It makes one super human and to look like not prone to any danger. Some of the leaders are church members but do not take heed of the church's role in their lives. Their developmental plans are based more on their human than divine drive. Human we are and have become such that when the proud fall, they go with most of their work because people will try as much as possible to destroy it least it reminds them of the person.

To come out of pride and move to reality is by first knowing the indicators of pride and the dangers involved. Know that the moment you see yourself better than others and deserve the best positioning in your community or work place, then know you are heading for "Pride". It is true that at work places, we are differently placed but as in the narrative of the house mentioned earlier, we work together for the beauty of that work. The church therefore needs to seek for Life-Giving Resources, which can improve and restore human dignity as well as their work values and working relationships to produce sustainable development. There is always a turning point and an opportunity to change from our pride to humility. Three things can help us turn around and change from pride to humility, from conventional to sustainable development. The church is an institution, through which restoration can be realized, and of all the responsibilities, the church can carry out; restoration is primary.

30. The Economic Challenge to Sustainable Development

The major focus towards the church's role in sustainable development is primarily an economic issue, which denies the church from providing spiritual resources to her people. The economic demands tend to submerge the spiritual values, and whether we are at low or high levels of the social setting, the love of money has always been a strong challenge to seeing the right cause for sustainable development. There are specific areas that can guide us to this economic challenge.

31. The Ecological Picture Through the Building Industry

In countries like Uganda, there have been challenges caused by unemployment. To meet the everyday needs, some of the people have resorted to doing some innovations in order to make a leaving. Some have turned to agriculture, others to building industry by engaging in sand mining and brick making. Every time there is an innovation, there must be a necessity of carrying out an environmental impact assessment. Unfortunately, sand mining and brick making which constitute major raw materials required for local building industry have continuously been exploited without taking in account how much havoc they are causing to our environment. Environmental Management Authorities might have been put in place just as a cover up, while behind the curtains, business has been going on with no due considerations of the negative impact. If it has been done, the truth has remained hidden.

People are mining sand and making bricks at will, without following any regulation or having environment enforcement authorities to guide them. It is good to engage in work and avoid poverty, redundancy, begging, and stealing, but also on the other hand to understand the value of what we engage in. Some of these innovations are generating money for those people as part of development, but are highly threatening the environment and human existence. People living a long major rivers in Uganda like river Rwizi in Greater Ankole region, Mpanga in the greater Rwenzori region, Nyamwamba in Kasese, Manafwa in Mbale, and many others, have been involved in a lot of sand mining and brick making for construction industry. While the construction industry is booming, the environment that supplies the raw materials is being depleted. People are earning a lot of money from these projects and therefore the ability to see the degradation they are causing has been blindfolded by the income they generate. People engaged in the construction industry are mostly well-paid government officers, some of whom are policy makers but cannot put a ban because they will stand to lose.

It must be noted that none of these projects is operated without affecting other habitats. For example, sand mining affects water catchment or basin and later it will cause floods during heavy rains and for people living in such areas would be negatively affected. A number of water creatures will also be adversely affected. For brick making, a similar hazard is likely to occur depending on how extensively the project is done, on addition to depleting forest cover while cutting wood for baking bricks. All these have both shot and long-term effects on humanity and the rest of the habitat. Both natural and planted forests are cut down to bake bricks by the building industry, and since the project is progressively encouraged by the booming industry, and forests are not being replanted, we can imagine where we are heading not far from today. Environment is the basic requirement for sustainable life, but if it is degraded, human beings will instead become one of the topmost endangered species. The process of sand mining and brick making has resulted into degrading rivers causing a lot of siltation, narrowing the rivers, and rising their beds so shallow that they cannot hold big volumes of water during heavy rains, thus causing destructive floods, while during drought they cannot hold up enough water for a larger population. The cutting down of trees for baking bricks, has also left the ground surface "naked". The environmentalists have assessed these trends as leading to the drying out of some of the rivers, while others have caused unforgettable and unforgivable landslides and floods threatening human and animal life; a case in point is Bududda at the slopes of Mount Elgon regions. Whereas on one side people would see it as a means of doing projects for earning a livelihood, the question should be; for how long? Is that kind of innovation sustainable for all? Even the few beneficiaries will not depend on this kind of work for generations because sand and clay will eventually be depleted completely, leaving behind nothing. When the rivers dry up, the people will suffer. The question keeps coming up; how sustainable are these economic developments? Does the church have any spiritual resource that can guide developers and innovators? Yes, I believe so, because the church is God's voice in the world he created for the good of his creation. God said, "let us create man in our image and own likeness so that they may rule over..." Man's rulership is based on God's wisdom to sustain the universe in the process of usage. The church has the role to teach people their responsibilities while they are making different developmental decisions and projects. In fact Christian education should be the means by which knowledge should be passed on to the people who care to learn their responsibilities as they engage in development. Development is not inclined to one particular variable; instead, it is a projection or planning of what we want it to be for now and tomorrow. The assumption would be that it would bear successful results showing progression or sustainability. In that case, development can be addressed as 'positive progresses'. We need direction if we want to realize this type of development for us and for our next generations. We can look at three examples through which we can assess the impact of peoples' engagements in development.

Picture 7: The degraded river

32. The Theological Interpretation

Every developmental engagements we do here on earth have or must have a theological dimension that would translate its importance within our beliefs and practices. It must have a religious value to all creation. The understanding of what we do or not do depends on our understanding of our God and his creation through the Scriptures. Grudem says;

Development strategies are intended for Christian leaders who believe the Bible and are willing to follow its principles for economic development, and we are writing to leaders, because they are the ones who can bring about the necessary change in their countries…because their preaching and teaching can eventually change a culture.[48]

The responsibility laid upon Christian leaders is so much entrenched in the church membership once they are given the teaching and preaching from well-informed and competent leaders. The understanding above is that whenever the church leadership stands to preach and teach, they must bring out the biblical truth about development. They have the capacity to develop or under develop their churches and countries, and indeed many of them have caused a lot of environmental derision simply because either they do not know what to say or do, or possibly, they fear because of pointing a finger against their financial sponsors. It is really a big assignment to undertake which even other professional stakeholders in development cannot devalue. Therefore, the church has the full responsibility to see to it that the biblical religious truth is taught and there is meaningful sustainable development not to her institution alone but to the entire nation. The theology of interdependence[49] is an important aspect of life. Every creation is dependent on each other, no matter the degree of dependence. Besides, there is the theology of co-existence. Creation lives alongside each other in harmony without causing the extinction or suffocation of the other. This then becomes the core of sustainable development in a world of demand and supply in a market of spiritual deficit. Development should not be left only to be a matter of the head, the classroom, the book or the black/white board, but also a matter of the heart that will connect to the master developer, who is God. Anything done outside God's mandate will be short lived because it will lack endorsement.

---

[48] Wyne Grudem and Barry Asmus, *The Poverty of Nations: A Sustainable solution* (Wheaton, Illinois: Crossway, 2013), p. 31.

[49] B.T. Adeney's article in the *New Dictionary of Christian Ethics & Pastoral Theology* (Nottingham, England: IVP,1995) p.104.

The creation of the universe by a supreme God followed by the guide lines on how human beings can utilize the environment are so theological that unless we understand our roles as human beings towards God's creation, our mandate as God's stewards will fail. The theology of maintaining our environment is another way of maintaining and sustaining ourselves, because it determines our earthly fate. The shorter or longer the development programs will last, the productivity will prove to be worth the benefits, and definitely, that will be determined by our sensitivity to the environmental usage. When God spoke out to human beings that they; "subdue but also replenish" (Gen.1:28 RSV), he was focusing on the way how life could be sustained at the hands of its users and beneficiaries, well knowing that mismanagement would bring about unsustainability and life would be in danger. A case in point are the frequent floods experienced almost everywhere in the world. Draught has also been widely experienced, causing food shortages and deaths. From the dimension of experience mentioned earlier, the pictures are intended to show us the extent of neglect and degradation of the earth without a sense of replenishing it for future sustainability of the next generations. God aware of the fact that it was important to preserve our environment, had even directed the Israelites to give the land a complete one year's rest so that it can rejuvenate and become productive for the next six years (Leviticus 25:1-7). That in itself was intended to give the land an ability of continuous productivity. At that time, we may say that the population was small and industries also were very few that there was no high demand for extensive use of sand, clay and trees that would degrade the land. Whereas it is true that the world cannot develop without exploiting her resources, it is also true to say that the resources must be exploited wisely, well knowing that we are not the last of human generations. Life is co-existent and interdependent with a long-range focus. We do not live as if today is the final day. Yes, it may be true for some but not for all. God did not initially create trees for brick baking, neither sand for building. Nevertheless, thank God for human beings becoming so innovative to construct houses and other types of physical infrastructures to sustain life. One important factor of life that we should not overlook is that no single life should be exploited or exterminated on the expense of the other. There must be a reasonable balance to justify the co-existence and inter-dependence factors. If the trend of irresponsible development continued as it were today, the next generation would end in complete impasse. Life must be lived in respect of creation even if some creation must serve the other, there must be a considerate and realistic balance in the utilization of resources available. Today in Uganda there is sand mining from Lake Victoria. Because of lack of theological inquest by the miners and even the Government, very few people are bothered to know the future repercussion. When we are all gone, there will be no one to sympathize with our grandchildren as the hostility created by our present developmental programs begins to pinch them hard. Why did God create rivers, lakes, seas and oceans with sand beds? Why did he also create off shore sand mines? He knew that human beings would need it for construction without going into the waters. Someone asked a question we could think through for the construction industry. The question was; why cannot builders import sand from Sahara and Kalahari deserts where there is too much sand in order to save rivers and lakebeds? That question may not be for you or me as church members, but for investors to explore. Perhaps it might have been tested and found lacking or some good reasons might be that Africans are too poor to import such an expensive commodity, but also important to not, is that desert sand is another environmental cover that God intended for that particular part of the world. Where do desert people get their building materials? That is one question among many asked, but we can think through and see if there is sense to construct an agenda to use alternative means to saving the dying rivers and lakes.

The Egyptian Pyramids were constructed with non-baked bricks. They have existed since around the year 2600 B.C. Imagine each Pyramid required baked bricks, how much wood would have been required, or forest would have been cut down to bake those bricks. The Pyramid is an example of telling us that big structures can be built using non-baked bricks.[50] Today, there is the technology of using soil and cement to make instant building blocks/bricks. How far that can work, is a matter of continued experimentation, but it can be used for the construction of single or two story houses, which are common in the developing countries. We may not think the ancient Egyptian way today, because technology has changed so much, but also with it has come environmental challenges. However, it would have been good enough for such technologies to provide ways of sustaining and maintaining our environment. The biblical theology helps us as church people to make note of very serious and fundamental issues when thinking of sustainability and development. When God created, he saw everything good and endorsed it for continuous existence. There are no ways for us, who have been given responsibility as caretakers, to turn around and despise the credible creativity of God by denying its continuous existence. Taking you back to the science of creation, sand, clay, water and trees or green vegetation, all have specific functions in human and animal life. I will not go scientific or experimental, but we must be aware of the fact that trees and green cover are good filters of air and sunrays for human life. They are also important in the formation of rain. If they were not there, then life would be at the brink of extinction or completely wiped out, especially human life. Clay soils are very important for holding up water for

---

[50] The earliest known Egyptian Pyramids are found at Saqqara, Northwest of Memphis (2630-2611 B.C). By 2008, there were between 118 and 138 Pyramids still in existence. The largest of the Pyramids measured 755.75 ft. (230 meters) at the base, and 481.4 ft. (147 meters) high. This would be the equivalent of a modern building of 44 to 48 stories.

our use. Areas where the clay layer is very thin or non-existent, people experience water shortages and long dry spells. When we dig out clay, we reduce catchment capacity and storage sustainability because water will run away since there will be nothing to hold it up. Areas where there are very thin clay soils, if brick making became extensively dominant, without any doubt people would face water problems. Sand and swamps are good filters of water from dangerous toxins. In addition, the two help to provide habitation for some aquatic animals, some of which we are supplied with food. Removing sand from the river banks, beds and lake shores has got two dangers; (i) it allows in siltation that destroys the bed and becomes so shallow that cannot hold enough water leading to drying. (ii) It encourages floods during heavy rains, which threaten human and animal life. When God was creating, he gave each creation a boundary to avoid uncontrolled interaction disaster. So when human beings engage in unchecked development, they end up causing chaos and destruction of life like it were, and is in Bududa area on Mt. Elgon in Uganda a decade ago. Therefore, the theology of creation is a subject the church should endeavor to teach her members and help developers to improve on their development plans to sustain life. Most of the people engaged in local and advanced sand mining, brick making and baking, are Christians who go to different churches though, but with the ability to understand what the Scriptures say about their creation mandate. The church has the mandate to speak divinely and authoritatively against destructive development, with the ability to give better options to what is currently done. The spiritual resources are available to help every church member to think and do, not only with a focus of individualism but rather collectivism.

"Biblical theology" and "theology of work" are like an operating system to revive a dying person. They have tools to bring life into the dying work values and making development meaningful to all. However, they draw their authority from God. They portray God's centrality and the importance of the work, which was assigned to us. Any "development" that does not recognize the hand of God is not worth the venture. God created all human beings equal with the capacity to perform when he delegated them responsibilities. All people have the potentials of doing one thing or the other, may be at the same time or different times. That is why when one leaves; another one comes in and sometimes performs much better than the predecessor did. Season come seasons go, so are human beings as the writer of Ecclesiastes tells us that everything has its own time. In other words, theology reveals that all of us are performers much as we may not be equal in our successes or our failures. It is only God, who works within us, that makes us able to achieve his goals and not our goals. We have no goals because we never set out for any. If the work we are doing were ours, then it would make sense to say that we have achieved our goals, but when our work becomes successful, God appreciates because we would have reached the mark set for us. Theology of work helps us as we work to discover the why, what, when and how questions. When they are answered then we would know the importance of our work in the local and global, but most importantly in God's developmental plans. The Bible is a good resource to unveil the hidden treasures of developmental work. The church must have the ability to explore this theology for her members so that they can direct their work towards sustainable development. It is one thing to work and another to work well and sustain it. What the church must do and do it willingly and ably is to teach her members to always be in the lead of others as they work basing on the Socratic method of dialogue. Human beings are known for their failures, but God in his divine wisdom has provided ways out as to keep life going in spite of those failures.

33. Traditional Beliefs and Practices

Different people have different traditions. In this section we shall take a look at a few that people cherish and ignorantly promote without seeing the negative impact such traditions have on sustainable development. In most communities, some traditions have been found to be non-compliant with life giving resources. If we take an example of people looking for virgin land because of its fertility and likelihood to support bumper harvest, they go for forests, cut them down and go ahead to put in fire, with a belief that when vegetation is burnt, it becomes very productive. Fire is one of the most destructive enemies of soil nutrients in that bush fires burn at higher temperatures that destroy the best of the needed soils for cultivation. Later when the ground "blanket" has been destroyed, three things happen that will continuously affect the future developments as long as the tradition is continued from one year to another.

- ➢ There will be severe weathering caused by direct sunshine and winds.
- ➢ Whenever there will be rain, it will run off with most of the top soil denying the soil to recover its natural blanket especially if the terrain is slopping.
- ➢ The soils will be over cultivated or over used resulting in poor productivity.

Therefore, what do we learn from the experience about people's traditions? Where we live and work are good learning centers of human activities, and since the church is a people based institution, she must engage her members in learning these crucial matters that affect development. As we engage work and work with others, the reality of who we are will always show up. We have seen people rise and fall, and others coming from nowhere to somewhere. Some of those who fall do so because of sticking to noncompliant traditions towards sustainable practices. Personal neglect of conducive traditions leads to absorption into destructive actions. Timely caution should be taken seriously before things turn against us when we are still here on earth. At some earliest point in time, we might have known the truth but never cared to mend. An old adage that says; "A stitch in time saves a nine" is a good a caution that many help us to be on our guard.

The traditional belief in all cultures is that we live by our work. We were born workers, and we shall die the same because we live by the works of our hands. We must work and live as community. One works within the tradition found in a home and the community, and no one is rewarded better in every day's work than others if he or she has been engaged in work, unless the products of his or her work are anti- human. To continue the culture of work, we must aim at sustainable work that will serve future generations after us. Otherwise, the cultivator should not be treated much better than the herds' man should, and the builder, no less than the village chief should. All will converge at a meal because in one way or the other, they have a contribution through what they do to the family and community life. Whoever defies intrinsic work is not worth the benefits of others who work. Traditionally no one was expected to see himself or herself more of a worker than others or to work for others. From childhood everybody grew in the culture of work and grew knowing that, work determined the wellbeing of an individual. Noteworthy is that the Jewish tradition did not violate this understanding. Paul used the same understanding to reproach the Thessalonians who waited idly for the coming of Jesus Christ, cautioning them that those who did not work should not eat (…). One must eat what he or she has labored for; after all, we must eat out of our sweat and not out of others sweat. We engage develop for our own dependence but also for those around us and those coming after us. After wards, others will continue or add on the same foundation. If we leave behind a shaky foundation, it will not remain for long before it will be destroyed. Let us mind about how we work. The church has a very rich tradition that helps her members to make work in all its dimensions God driven.

VI

MORAL HINDRANCES TO SUSTAINABLE DEVELOPMENT

Greed: This is a desire to have more than one requires, but also a feeling that when others get, one may miss out, and as a result, one may end up rushing for something he has no capacity to hold on to. Some people fight hard to get too much possession without the techniques of how to maintain it. They have the hearts full of dissatisfaction. Greed is one of the all-time cross-borders vices of most people. It can be greed for possession of power, property, food, status and so on and so forth. Greed, like pride does not have boundaries. Greed is one of those vices, which can interfere with well-intended development. It aims at satisfying self than others. It is not development friendly. Greed has destroyed individuals of high status, nations of great acclaim and has gone as far as s destroying economies and political blocks. As if that is normal, greed has not spared spiritual leaders. Work places are good conduits for greed because there is a lot of competition for a number of things. At planning tables, greed sits in silence waiting to see where the decision is directed. It sits among high-ranking people, people with very moving ideas, and on the surface, it will always appear workable, and will seem to hurt nobody or even benefit specific individuals. When it erupts, it endangers people's lives because the moment it does not get what it wants, in most cases it will hunt down those who had taken advantage over it. It burns in people's hearts as an inflaming passion to possess more than what others have. It kills the goodness in most people. It looks more at taking than giving. Greed does not allow most of us to appreciate what God has given us no matter how much compared to what others have. That is how greed grows and affects well-intended development because of its self-seeking behavior. It does not sustain the common good for all but instead looks out for all possible outlets to grab what appears to be "opportunities" for the few against the many less powerful. It does not respect private or public interests as long as its long arm can distort the intended good. It becomes worse when it runs a syndicate of well-informed and influential people. The world over, powerful and influential people who are rich, have been known for destroying the developmental goals that would have supported and sustained many others.

We sometimes use work as a means to accumulate wealth at the expense of others. You will find many people having multiple employments while others have nothing at all, because the greed for money works behind all our intentions and as a result, we cause employment deficiency, which eventually affects the moral behaviors of those who are not employed or working for a pay. Greed changes people's behaviors and appearances. Some behave like a pouncing lion and others like a diving eagle especially when the need has been so long suppressed and the opportunity seem to avail itself without legal restrictions.[51] Workplaces are common fields where most of these are experienced. They find favor in and with public places and are less noticeable when alone but you must know that even when people are alone, they can be tempted to think that they do not have enough to themselves. When not checked, greedy people can cause fights, displacements, envy, enmity, jealousy and hatred, wastages, loses and deaths. What more, it can destroy personality beyond recovery.

---

[51] Legal is something to do with the law. If we say legal restrictions, we are saying that greed has no law to challenge it because in most cases it is within the person's heart. It is a type of covetousness.

In the event of thinking and doing development, when greed is allowed to find favor among development planners and developers, without doubt, the outcome will not be sustainable. It will more likely serve a few or end up serving none because of its non-existence because greed swallowed it. Where there is greed, there are hawk like people ready to dive and take advantage of development resources. If any development is put in place, the greedy will try as best as they can to utilize it for their own benefits. There are many examples of African leaders, who turned or have turned public utilities into personal utilities even when they have been well facilitated by their government. The kind of behavior does not sustain the economy optimally and it denies the public to enjoy the facilities intended for their services.

To overcome greed, we must above all be contented with what we have and appreciate God given resources set before us. We must see all developments for the public good and encourage ourselves to aim at the best ways of benefiting from them.

34. Lust

Like all other silent killers, lust is another deadly hitch that can destroy character before destroying work. It first kills personality and later moves on to destroy other people without giving them opportunities to know what is steaming up before they discover that they have been webbed up. Lust is encouraged by sight, and mind (thinking). It is greed in abstract. Sight is a very strong influence of what people like or hate most. Sight sends signals into the brain, and imaginations begin to form up towards what it would be like, if something happened. One might not necessarily be in need of anything, but greed and lust might push him or her. The most common destructive lust is the lust of possession and position, common in work places. Once it develops among workmates, it destroys work values and sound productivity. One notable thing we must all know is that lust is human. Every normal human being experiences lust but it is a negative force socially and spiritually that fails us. It destroys our character and work. King David had lust for Bathsheba, wife of Uriah, and his heart run mad and he ended up sleeping with her. He destroyed his character and relationship with God. Lust had denied him from going to war with Israel's armies. Have you ever asked yourself what led King Solomon to marrying one thousand wives? What about King Ahab and Naboth's vineyard? Did it ever occur to you why most of the ancient empires sought to control nations of the world? What about present super powers? Possession and position were, and are the driving forces. In this case, lust has no particular home. Someone said that the rich and well-placed people have a high feel of lust than their minors. Well I do not know, but the statement tells us that lust cuts across all lifestyles despite the varying degrees and ages. The lust of King David and Solomon did not sustain a smooth relationship with God, and later it left remarkable negative marks on their lives and families. Solomon's relationship with God was not sustainable to the extent that after his death, the kingdom was divided. When we let lust control us, most of our social, religious, political and economic developments become unsustainable.

Another case is of Bill Clinton, the American president, who inside the White House fell victim of his uncontrolled lust and had sexual relations with a White House intern; Lewinsky. I do not want to overstretch the issue because we all know how sex is a strong influence to lust and have destroyed many high-profile personalities behind great developmental projects. Even you and I, at one time might have been hooked up. You see lust is a heart and brain matter and, in most cases,, it is hard to tell who has it if not unleashed to those round you. Many people do have lust, but their experiences are never shared, and since lust is abstract, there is no better word to define it at its best except when it manifests itself into deeds. However, the point advanced here is that this kind of lust once found at work places, it would destroy many values. It pushes many to speak and even act contrary to the wishes of their vic-tims. Administrative roles will be undermined; insubordination will become the workplace experience, what else? Productivity, harmony, respect and dignity will be lost. Lust is a silent killer that destroys leadership roles, human values and development goals.

In sustainable development, there is another side of lust that kills work and workplace joy and that is lust for money. People love money more than they love work. They will spend more time moving about pretending to be working and looking for money but doing less work. There is a saying that people want to make ends meet; meaning that they have to look for sources of money in order to meet their needs and even accumulate riches. In this process, lust for money leads many workers to hold more than one job. In the normal circumstances, none of any of those jobs will be perfectly done because the mind runs to all the other jobs already acquired. One must try to show ones presence even when nothing is being done. At the end of the month, one will get payment for all the jobs even if nothing has been registered in performance as longer as one has been seen present.

One of the major things many of us workers have not grasped right is that what we earn is not the determinant of what we do, but rather that what we do should determine what we should earn. Whether that makes sense to us or not, some of us fill comfortable with it because we earn from different unscrupulous sources where we have not done any work to be paid for. Lust for money is the best killer of development and quality assurance, procurement protocols, and above all the spirituality of work.

Places where lust for sex and money has been involved; we will find that there are personality and workplace crises. It does not matter whether you are a Christian or not, but the point is that as long as you are human and a public worker, you will be affected together with your workplace. We do not cease to live humanly because of where we work or what our faiths are. There are people who are able to control their lust, but then those around them whose control is low, will make their working environment resentful. It is like a good and careful driver who is crashed by the bad and careless driver; because both are on the same road. How then can we avoid this silent personality and work killer? God in his way knows our human weaknesses, and he has provided means to overcome it. We need to control our human desires as he had warned Cain (Gen.4:6, 7).

35. Anger

Deprivation of happiness. Usually caused by disappointments; insults, shame, failures or even sickness. When one is angry, it affects the work in and out puts because the spirit of work becomes distorted and the heart's focus is on the source of anger. Some people have been known to cry, fail to eat and even speak because of anger. How then would one expect an angry person to be a good worker? We have witnessed most workers who translate their family anger into workplace anger. Every work appears to be the cause of that person's anger. If it is the boss, then be prepared to face hell every time he/she comes to work angry. The workplace will become a battlefield of psychological and social wars, to which most workers will become victims of circumstances. To know that anger is dangerous, it destroys hearing capacity because the angry person listens to himself or herself. The mind is far from the present and goes back in the past where anger originated. Anger deceives some people that they are strong and can defy anybody or even fight him or her. Instructions are overlooked. Because of anger, what could have been done rightly and timely will be left unattended to. Anger defies many respects. Managers must know what causes anger in the work places. In families, couple must know the source of anger in order to find its cure in good time. In order to overcome anger, we can choose to do the following or leave them to our own peril.

36. Laziness

A condition of unwillingness to work, doing little or nothing yet the person has all the potentials and resources to work. It is lack of effort or care to do anything, or it is a slow undertaking when strength and effort are expected. It can be described as a pathological busyness or unreasonably busy for nothing. Many people, who are lazy, do little work compared to the resources they have. When they choose to work, they look for the less important work because they love ease. Paul and Alvin have likened lazy people to a three-toed sloth in the Amazon that hangs upside down from the branches and moves so sluggishly that moss grows on its sun-drenched belly.[52] This might translate into lazy people who slouch up, and in bemused indifference neglecting their worthwhile talents to lay a waste. Where they sit, their foot stamps have made the ground hardened because of over stepping, and the seat of their buttocks heats up like an oven. When assigned work, their laziness tells them to avoid what appears difficult, or too engaging, with many excuses resulting in more work for their fellow workers. Look around yourself; do not you see people whose work habits are like the character of a sloth? Donald Trump once a real estate mogul, and now the president of United States of America reacted: "There are few things I hate more than laziness, I work very, very hard and I expect the people who work for me to do the same. If you want to succeed, you cannot relax…"[53] Clearly the slothful or lazy people are less successful. However, Paul and Alvin argue that lazy people are not the only ones who are slow but that extremely busy people can also be slouch. For example, workaholics tend to have symptoms of family neglect. They love their work on the ex-

---

[52] Paul Stevens and Alvin Ung, *Taking Your Soul to Work* (USA: Eerdmans Publishing House, 2009), p.30.

[53] Donald J. Trump, *The Fifth Deadly Workplace Sin: Sloth,* The Trump Blog, entry posted October 10, 2007, http://www.trumpuniversity.com/blog/2007/10/the-fifth-deadly-workplace-sin-sloth.cfm (accessed May 12, 2018).

pense of their families, and become very slow to respond to signals of neglected love from family members because they are self- absorbed. They feel for nothing else other than their work 24/7. If ever they do come home and seem to be present physically, their whole minds are at their workstations and desks. This should not sound confusing. Remember your strength in one area of life cannot make up for your great weakness in another area. The "dew point" comes when such people come to realize that what they were supposed to do personally have piled up beyond manageable size. Sustainable public developmental engagements do not necessarily sustain families, and the opposite is true. When blame, guilty and depression begin to set in and we begin to resent, know for sure that the engagements are not sustainable for either family or public developments. Some workers sometimes are called before their bosses to answer for unfinished assignments. Some men and women are tasked to answer why they are lazy at their family responsibilities. In this case never praise yourself for pleasing your boss and work mates and you forget pleasing your spouse and children. Every kind of work requires active mind, body and spirit. We cannot have them at equal degrees, but our response to them must be positive and productive.

However, Derek Kidner asserts that the lazy also work, by saying that they never begin, never finish things and never face up to things. Such people prefer to whittle away at less problems while refusing to attend to the most important work at hand. Therefore, they become restless with dissatisfied longing, helpless in the face of the jumble of their affairs.[54] The most disturbing is that they deny themselves active engagement to do what they know they must do (Pro. 21:25-26). When we experience laziness at workplaces, we are likely to see the following behaviors among those affected.

---

[54] Derek Kidner, *The Proverbs: An Introduction and Commentary* (Chicago: Inter-Varsity Press, 1975), pp. 42-43.

1. Drifters from one amusement to another. They loathe the daily tediousness of work. They feel the best of their enjoyment in life is endless where there is no stress, no pain or anxiety and no objective decision to influence action except eating and drinking, and finding the easy side of life.

2. Some people work sluggishly during the day, but seek for incentives to life as soon as they leave their workstations and sometimes enter places of worship. They refuse intentionally to invest fully in the workplace, claiming their jobs are secular, yet they can pay their daily bills but they have no Godly-serving attitude. If the worker is a Christian, he/she must have the working heart of God and Christ.

3. Some workers simply work for a salary and do not want to make any difference as they work. They are physically present but their minds are set somewhere else. They are therefore not concerned about what is happening; they are not involved, not committed and not caring. Whether others are working or not, wasteful or not, present or not; it is none of their business. People of that type demoralize their co-workers and take away their will and effort to the work they love.[55]

4. Workaholics who meet almost above 90% of work expectations, their pay off most likely is enviously huge. However, they have numerous hidden costs that might never be paid forever. Such extreme workers have been known never to have enough sleep and even exercises. They have few friends other than their work, computer and the four walls of their offices but not even their fellow workaholics. They are too reactive even against simple comments and are known to neglect relationships with their families. After their every day's heavy work,

---

[55] Dan Miller, *To The Work You Love* (Nashville, Tennessee: Broadman & Holman Publishers, 2005), p.10.

they are or feel too tired even to talk and hug their spouses. Their homes are a neglected lot. It will be years later, when they will no longer be in active service, probably retired, when they will look around for company and find none, because they never prepared for one. Their language is foreign to their new environment and it is too late to fix. It is not bad to be work-minded, but also it is not good to neglect those around you because they are the spice of you work life. Laziness or slothfulness to family life is not a guarantee to a successful work life. Frederick Buechner sees slothful people as; "...very busy people. They are people who...fly on automatic pilot. Like somebody with a bad head cold, they have mostly lost their sense of taste and smell. They know something is wrong with them, but not wrong enough to do anything about it."[56] In other words, they have the mind to think about other people's work and not to see their social and religious responsibilities.

To avoid being overrun by unnoticed slothfulness, we have to learn the long-term effects of laziness to our personal well- being, our communities and above all our Creator and take on the mind of some of Christ. It is Scriptural that laziness kills the relationship around us and ends up making us poor (Prov.).

37. Envy

Is a condition deep in the heart that commands the eyes to look at what others have, like you have, or do not have and it begins creating in you, the spirit of hatred and enemty. It has attendant cousins; jealousy, covetousness, and greed. It is a strong driving force against friendships or fellowships. At workplaces, it is mostly generated by positions or

---

[56] Frederick Buechner, *Wishful Thinking: A Seeker's ABC* (San Francisco: Harpers, 1993), pp.109-110.

status, appraisals in favor of fellow work mates, emoluments, and good working relationships with bosses, beauty and smartness, promotions, favorable postings, admirable academic credentials and many other work place dynamics. Envy is a disease that is hard to cure once it has been allowed to take place in ones heart unless one accepts to get a life-giving resource that can nourish the spirit.

Most workers are known to suffer from this kind of disease even without shame against their subordinates or juniors; as long as they have something good about them that they do not have. Most workers have been known to practice witchcraft, concoct or formulate false stories against those they envy so that they can be rid of them from the same work places. Others have been known to or want to cause the death to those they envy (Gen. 4:6; 37:2-27). Sometimes we fail to realize that those we envy are real assets to productive work and true manifestations of Christ-like character. If ever envy were allowed to excel, there would never be lucidity because it would subdue all truth and promote false-hood without any upward relationship. Our horizontal focus is the one that denies us to have the goodwill for others and love our work and ourselves as we are. If you ever hear fights at work places or what people call character assassinations, then know that the endemic disease called 'envy' is infesting itself among workers. The Spirituality of work is meant to check such diseases and cleanup for better working environment. Workplaces are spiritual mission centers where joy and happiness are experienced. When envy is allowed to find its seat there, then for sure soon or later you will register "the death of work" with all its front line players.

VII

SUGGESTIONS AND RECOMMENDATIONS

1. In order to realize environmental and sustainable development globally, the Church should teach the biblical truth about the theology of work and development in order to become a front-line participant and change agent.

2. The church should use the 'pulpit' to teach her members on matters concerning sustainable development, and encourage workers to engage their hands, heads and hearts in development programs.

3. Since many Christians are not English readers and speakers, development should not only be seen as an academic discipline. Since all humankind has a responsibility to protect the environment and work towards sustainable development, the church should engage the subject from a socio-religious perspective, before looking at its economic benefits.

VIII

CONCLUSION

Having an understanding of biblical and Christian theology helps Christians to understand their position in work and development. It guides them to trace work right from creation without undermining its values. The formulation of any meaningful theology, Christians must see the centrality of God and his creative work, in which they are main players of work and development. Consideration of the fall should be taken seriously to avoid its continued effects of undermining work values even when Jesus has liberated everything, including human work.

After the coming of Jesus Christ and his redemptive work, Christians should guard against remaining the same. The Bible makes it very clearly that all will be judged based on the result of works. Good work motivates one another towards acts of love (Heb.10:24). Christians should work towards making complete their final journey by doing Godly work influenced by the biblical teaching, not to themselves only, but also to others (Matt.5:16). Remembering that Christians are stewards placed in God's estate to work and develop it as he did for his glory. When Christians know that they are working for the glory of God they will find complete joy in developing their talents/gifts and all that have been entrusted to them.

Most of the developmental shortcomings are mostly caused by our human selfish gains. Although our work was corrupted by the fall, the coming of Jesus Christ has liberated everything including our work. Human beings cannot be liberated spiritually, and then are left to engage their work in corruption. In spite of our failures to engage sustainable development, our position can be improved on by relying on what the Bible teaches us, because it had all the basics required for our development sustainably.

38. Bibliography

Atkinson David J. et'la, *New Dictionary of Christian Ethics and Pastoral Theology.* Downers Grove, Illinois: IVP, 1995.

Bediako Kwame, *Christianity in Africa: The Renewal of non-Western Religion.* USA: Orbis Books, 1997.

Chambers Robert, *Ideas for Development.* London: Earthscan Publishers, 2005.

Child J. G. *Christian Reconstruction Movement (article) in the New Dictionary of Christian Ethics and Pastoral Theology.*Downers Grove, Illinois: IVP, 1995.

Gilbert C. Meilaender, (ed.) *Working: Its meaning and limits.* Notre Dame: university of Notre Dame Press, 2000.

Grudem Wayne. *Systematic Theology.* Leicester, England: IVP, 2000.

Higginson Richard. *Called to Account: Adding Value in God's World - Integrating Christianity and Business Effectively.* Guildford, Surrey: Eagle Publishers, 1993.

Hornby A.S Advanced *Learner's Dictionary.*Oxford: Oxford University Press, 2004.

Jenkins Philip. *The New Faces of Christianity.* New York: Oxford University Press, 2006.

Linthicum Robert. *Transforming Power: Biblical Strategies for Making Difference in Your Community.*Downers Grove, Illinois: IVP Books, 2003.

Miller Dan. *To the Work You Love.*Nashville, Tennessee: Broadman & Holman Publishers, 2005.

Pearce David et'al, *Sustainable Development: Economic and Environment in the Third World.* London: Earthscan Publishers, 1990.

Shepherd, Andrew. *Sustainable Rural Development.* New York: Palgrave, 1998.

Sikolia, Mulevi Suzan. *Development and African Christian Identity; The Case Study of the Catholic Church in Kakamega, Kenya.* An M.A Research Paper 1992.

Smith Oswald, *God's Judgement Day.* Belfast: every Home Crusade, 1980.

Stevens Paul, *Doing God's Business.*Grand Rapids, Michigan: William Eerdmans Publishing Company, 2006.

Volf Moroslav. *"Human work Divine Spirit, and the New Creation: Toward a Pneumatological understanding of work" Pneuma,* The Journal of the Society for Pentecostal Studies, Study.webcrawler.com, 1987, accessed 2020.

——, *Work in the Spirit: Towards a Theology of Work.* Oxford: Oxford University Press, 1991.

World Development Report, *A Better Investment Climate for Everyone: The International World Bank for Reconstruction and Development- WB.* New York: Oxford University Press, 2004.

Globethics.net Publications

The list below is only a selection of our publications. To view the full collection, please visit our website.

All free products are provided free of charge and can be downloaded in PDF form from the Globethics.net library and at www.globethics.net/publications. Bulk print copies can be ordered from *publictions@globethics.net* at special rates from the Global South.
Paid products not provided free of charge are indicated[*].
The Editor of the different Series of Globethics.net Publications Prof. Dr. Obiora Ike, Executive Director of Globethics.net in Geneva and Professor of Ethics at the Godfrey Okoye University Enugu/Nigeria.

Contact for manuscripts and suggestions: *publications@globethics.net*

Global Series

Christoph Stückelberger / Jesse N.K. Mugambi (eds.), *Responsible Leadership. Global and Contextual Perspectives*, 2007, 376pp. ISBN: 978–2–8254–1516–0

Heidi Hadsell / Christoph Stückelberger (eds.), *Overcoming Fundamentalism. Ethical Responses from Five Continents*, 2009, 212pp.
ISBN: 978–2–940428–00–7

Christoph Stückelberger / Reinhold Bernhardt (eds.): *Calvin Global. How Faith Influences Societies*, 2009, 258pp. ISBN: 978–2–940428–05–2.

Ariane Hentsch Cisneros / Shanta Premawardhana (eds.), *Sharing Values. A Hermeneutics for Global Ethics*, 2010, 418pp.
ISBN: 978–2–940428–25–0.

Deon Rossouw / Christoph Stückelberger (eds.), *Global Survey of Business Ethics in Training, Teaching and Research*, 2012, 404pp.
ISBN: 978–2–940428–39–7

Carol Cosgrove Sacks/ Paul H. Dembinski (eds.), *Trust and Ethics in Finance. Innovative Ideas from the Robin Cosgrove Prize*, 2012, 380pp.
ISBN: 978–2–940428–41–0

Jean-Claude Bastos de Morais / Christoph Stückelberger (eds.), *Innovation Ethics. African and Global Perspectives*, 2014, 233pp.
ISBN: 978–2–88931–003–6

Nicolae Irina / Christoph Stückelberger (eds.), *Mining, Ethics and Sustainability*, 2014, 198pp. ISBN: 978–2–88931–020–3

Philip Lee and Dafne Sabanes Plou (eds), *More or Less Equal: How Digital Platforms Can Help Advance Communication Rights*, 2014, 158pp. ISBN 978–2–88931–009–8

Sanjoy Mukherjee and Christoph Stückelberger (eds.) *Sustainability Ethics. Ecology, Economy, Ethics. International Conference SusCon III, Shillong/India*, 2015, 353pp. ISBN: 978–2–88931–068–5

Amélie Vallotton Preisig / Hermann Rösch / Christoph Stückelberger (eds.) *Ethical Dilemmas in the Information Society. Codes of Ethics for Librarians and Archivists*, 2014, 224pp. ISBN: 978–288931–024–1.

Prospects and Challenges for the Ecumenical Movement in the 21st Century. Insights from the Global Ecumenical Theological Institute, David Field / Jutta Koslowski, 256pp. 2016, ISBN: 978–2–88931–097–5

Christoph Stückelberger, Walter Fust, Obiora Ike (eds.), *Global Ethics for Leadership. Values and Virtues for Life*, 2016, 444pp. ISBN: 978–2–88931–123–1

Dietrich Werner / Elisabeth Jeglitzka (eds.), *Eco-Theology, Climate Justice and Food Security: Theological Education and Christian Leadership Development*, 316pp. 2016, ISBN 978–2–88931–145–3

Obiora Ike, Andrea Grieder and Ignace Haaz (Eds.), *Poetry and Ethics: Inventing Possibilities in Which We Are Moved to Action and How We Live Together*, 271pp. 2018, ISBN 978–2–88931–242–9

Christoph Stückelberger / Pavan Duggal (Eds.), *Cyber Ethics 4.0: Serving Humanity with Values*, 503pp. 2018, ISBN 978–2–88931–264–1

Theses Series

A. Halil Thahir, *Ijtihād Maqāṣidi: The Interconnected Maṣlaḥah-Based Reconstruction of Islamic Laws*, 2019, 200pp. ISBN 978-2-88931-220-7

Tibor Héjj, *Human Dignity in Managing Employees. A performative approach, based on the Catholic Social Teaching (CST)*, 2019, 320pp. ISBN 978-2-88931-280-1

Sabina Kavutha Mutisya, *The Experience of Being a Divorced or Separated Single Mother: A Phenomenological Study*, 2019, 168pp. ISBN 978-2-88931-274-0

Florence Muia, *Sustainable Peacebuilding Strategies. Sustainable Peacebuilding Operations in Nakuru County, Kenya: Contribution to the Catholic Justice and Peace Commission (CJPC)*, 2020, 195pp. ISBN 978-2-88931-331-0

Mary Rose-Claret Ogbuehi, *The Struggle for Women Empowerment Through Education*, 2020, 410pp. ISBN 978-2-88931-363-1

Texts Series

Principles on Sharing Values across Cultures and Religions, 2012, 20pp. Available in English, French, Spanish, German and Chinese. Other languages in preparation. ISBN: 978–2–940428–09–0

Ethics in Politics. Why it Matters More than Ever and How it Can Make a Difference. A Declaration, 8pp, 2012. Available in English and French. ISBN: 978–2–940428–35–9

Religions for Climate Justice: International Interfaith Statements 2008–2014, 2014, 45pp. Available in English. ISBN 978–2–88931–006–7

Ethics in the Information Society: The Nine 'P's. A Discussion Paper for the WSIS+10 Process 2013–2015, 2013, 32pp. ISBN: 978–2–940428–063–2

Principles on Equality and Inequality for a Sustainable Economy. Endorsed by the Global Ethics Forum 2014 with Results from Ben Africa Conference 2014, 2015, 41pp. ISBN: 978–2–88931–025–8

Water Ethics: Principles and Guidelines, 2019, 41pp. ISBN 978–2–88931-313-6

Éthique de l'eau: Principes et lignes directrices, 2019, 34pp. ISBN 978-2-88931-325-9

Ética del agua: Principios y directrices, 2020, 48pp. ISBN 978-2-88931-343-3

Focus Series

Christoph Stückelberger, *Das Menschenrecht auf Nahrung und Wasser. Eine ethische Priorität*, 2009, 80pp. ISBN : 978–2–940428–06–9

Christoph Stückelberger, *Corruption-Free Churches Are Possible. Experiences, Values, Solutions*, 2010, 278pp. ISBN: 978–2–940428–07–6

—, *Des Églises sans corruption sont possibles : Expériences, valeurs, solutions*, 2013, 228pp. ISBN : 978–2–940428–73–1

Vincent Mbavu Muhindo, *La République Démocratique du Congo en panne. Bilan 50 ans après l'indépendance*, 2011, 380pp. ISBN: 978–2–940428–29–8

Benoît Girardin, *Ethics in Politics: Why it matters more than ever and how it can make a difference*, 2012, 172pp. ISBN: 978–2–940428–21–2

—, *L'éthique : un défi pour la politique. Pourquoi l'éthique importe plus que jamais en politique et comment elle peut faire la différence*, 2014, 220pp. ISBN 978–2–940428–91–5

Willem A Landman, *End-of-Life Decisions, Ethics and the Law*, 2012, 136pp. ISBN: 978–2–940428–53–3

Corneille Ntamwenge, *Éthique des affaires au Congo. Tisser une culture d'intégrité par le Code de Conduite des Affaires en RD Congo*, 2013, 132pp. ISBN: 978–2–940428–57–1

Kitoka Moke Mutondo / Bosco Muchukiwa, *Montée de l'Islam au Sud-Kivu : opportunité ou menace à la paix sociale. Perspectives du dialogue islamo-chrétien en RD Congo*, 2012, 48pp.ISBN: 978–2–940428–59–5

Elisabeth Nduku / John Tenamwenye (eds.), *Corruption in Africa: A Threat to Justice and Sustainable Peace*, 2014, 510pp. ISBN: 978–2–88931–017–3

Dicky Sofjan (with Mega Hidayati), *Religion and Television in Indonesia: Ethics Surrounding Dakwahtainment*, 2013, 112pp. ISBN: 978–2–940428–81–6

Yahya Wijaya / Nina Mariani Noor (eds.), *Etika Ekonomi dan Bisnis: Perspektif Agama-Agama di Indonesia*, 2014, 293pp. ISBN: 978–2–940428–67–0

Bernard Adeney-Risakotta (ed.), *Dealing with Diversity. Religion, Globalization, Violence, Gender and Disaster in Indonesia*. 2014, 372pp. ISBN: 978–2–940428–69–4

Sofie Geerts, Namhla Xinwa and Deon Rossouw, EthicsSA (eds.), *Africans' Perceptions of Chinese Business in Africa A Survey*. 2014, 62pp. ISBN: 978–2–940428–93–9

Nina Mariani Noor/ Ferry Muhammadsyah Siregar (eds.), *Etika Sosial dalam Interaksi Lintas Agama* 2014, 208pp. ISBN 978–2–940428–83–0

Célestin Nsengimana, *Peacebuilding Initiatives of the Presbyterian Church in Post-Genocide Rwandan Society: An Impact Assessment*. 2015, 154pp. ISBN: 978–2–88931–044–9

Bosco Muchukiwa, *Identité territoriales et conflits dans la province du Sud-Kivu, R.D. Congo*, 53pp. 2016, ISBN: 978–2–88931–113–2

Dickey Sofian (ed.), Religion, *Public Policy and Social Transformation in Southeast Asia*, 2016, 288pp. ISBN: 978–2–88931–115–6

Symphorien Ntibagirirwa, *Local Cultural Values and Projects of Economic Development: An Interpretation in the Light of the Capability Approach*, 2016, 88pp. ISBN: 978–2–88931–111–8

Karl Wilhelm Rennstich, *Gerechtigkeit für Alle. Religiöser Sozialismus in Mission und Entwicklung*, 2016, 500pp. ISBN 978–2–88931–140–8.

John M. Itty, *Search for Non-Violent and People-Centric Development*, 2017, 317pp. ISBN 978–2–88931–185–9

Florian Josef Hoffmann, *Reichtum der Welt—für Alle Durch Wohlstand zur Freiheit*, 2017, 122pp. ISBN 978–2–88931–187–3

Cristina Calvo / Humberto Shikiya / Deivit Montealegre (eds.), *Ética y economía la relación dañada*, 2017, 377pp. ISBN 978–2–88931–200–9

Maryann Ijeoma Egbujor, *The Relevance of Journalism Education in Kenya for Professional Identity and Ethical Standards*, 2018, 141pp. ISBN 978–2–88931233–7

Christoph Stückelberger, *Globalance. Ethics Handbook for a Balanced World Post-Covid*, Geneva: Globethics.net, 2020, 617pp. ISBN 978-2-88931-367-9

Praxis Series

Christoph Stückelberger, *Responsible Leadership Handbook : For Staff and Boards*, 2014, 116pp. ISBN :978-2-88931-019-7 (Available in Russian)

Christoph Stückelberger, *Weg-Zeichen: 100 Denkanstösse für Ethik im Alltag*, 2013, 100pp SBN: 978-2-940428-77-9

—, *Way-Markers: 100 Reflections Exploring Ethics in Everyday Life*, 2014, 100pp. ISBN 978-2-940428-74-0

Nina Mariani Noor (ed.) *Manual Etika Lintas Agama Untuk Indonesia*, 2015, 93pp. ISBN 978-2-940428-84-7

Christoph Stückelberger, *Weg-Zeichen II: 111 Denkanstösse für Ethik im Alltag*, 2016, 111pp. ISBN: 978-2-88931-147-7 (Available in German and English)

Elly K. Kansiime, *In the Shadows of Truth: The Polarized Family*, 2017, 172pp. ISBN 978-2-88931-203-0

Oscar Brenifier, *Day After Day 365 Aphorisms*, 2019, 395pp. ISBN 978-2-88931-272-6

Christoph Stückelberger, *365 Way-Markers*, 2019, 416pp. ISBN: 978-2-88931-282-5 (Available in English and German).

Benoît Girardin / Evelyne Fiechter-Widemann (Eds.), *Blue Ethics: Ethical Perspectives on Sustainable, Fair Water Resources Use and Management,* forthcoming 2019, 265pp. ISBN 978-2-88931-308-2

Benoît Girardin / Evelyne Fiechter-Widemann (Eds*.), Éthique de l'eau: Pour un usage et une gestion justes et durables des ressources en eau,* 2020, 309pp. ISBN 978-2-88931-337-2

Didier Ostermann, *Le rôle de l'Église maronite dans la construction du Liban : 1500 ans d'histoire, du Ve au XXe siècle,* 2020, 142pp. ISBN 978-2-88931-365-5

African Law Series

D. Brian Dennison/ Pamela Tibihikirra-Kalyegira (eds.), *Legal Ethics and Professionalism. A Handbook for Uganda,* 2014, 400pp. ISBN 978–2–88931–011–1

Pascale Mukonde Musulay, *Droit des affaires en Afrique subsaharienne et économie planétaire,* 2015, 164pp. ISBN: 978–2–88931–044–9

Pascal Mukonde Musulay, *Démocratie électorale en Afrique subsaharienne : Entre droit, pouvoir et argent,* 2016, 209pp. ISBN 978–2–88931–156–9

Agape Series

崔万田 Cui Wantian *爱+经济学 Agape Economics,* 2020, 420pp. IBSN: 978-2-88931-349-5

Cui Wantian, Christoph Stückelberger, *The Better Sinner: A Practical Guide on Corruption,* 2020, 37pp. ISBN 978-2-88931-339-6. Available also in Chinese.

Anh Tho Andres Kammler, *FaithInvest: Impactful Cooperation. Report of the International Conference Geneva 2020,* 2020, 70pp. ISBN: 978-2-88931- 357-0

China Christian Series

Spirituality 4.0 at the Workplace and FaithInvest - Building Bridges, 2019, 107pp. ISBN 978-2-88931-304-4

海茵兹•吕格尔 / 克里斯多夫•芝格里斯特 (Christoph Sigrist/ Heinz Rüegger) *Diaconia: An Introduction. Theological Foundation of Christian Service,* 2019, 433pp. ISBN: 978-2-88931-302-0

Faith-Based Entrepreneurs Stronger Together. Report of the International Conference Geneva 2018, 2018, 86pp. ISBN: 978-2-88931-258-0

China Ethics Series

Liu Baocheng/Chandni Patel, *Overseas Investment of Chinese Enterprises. A Casebook on Corporate Social Responsibility*, forthcoming 2020, ISBN: 978-2-88931-355-6.

Liu Baocheng / Zhang Mengsha, *CSR Report on Chinese Business Overseas Operations*, 2018, 286pp. ISBN: 978-2-88931-250-4

刘宝成（Liu Baocheng）/ 张梦莎（Zhang Mengsha），中国企业"走出去"社会责任研究报告, 2018, 267pp. ISBN: 978-2-88931-248-1

Education Ethics Serie

Divya Singh / Christoph Stückelberger (Eds.), *Ethics in Higher Education Values-driven Leaders for the Future*, 2017, 367pp. ISBN: 978–2–88931–165–1

Obiora Ike / Chidiebere Onyia (Eds.) *Ethics in Higher Education, Foundation for Sustainable Development*, 2018, 645pp. IBSN: 978-2-88931-217-7

Obiora Ike / Chidiebere Onyia (Eds.) *Ethics in Higher Education, Religions and Traditions in Nigeria* 2018, 198pp. IBSN: 978-2-88931-219-1

Obiora F. Ike, Justus Mbae, Chidiebere Onyia (Eds.), *Mainstreaming Ethics in Higher Education: Research Ethics in Administration, Finance, Education, Environment and Law Vol. 1*, 2019, 779pp. ISBN 978-2-88931-300-6

Education Praxis Series*

Tobe Nnamani / Christoph Stückelberger, *Resolving Ethical Dilemmas in Profes-sional and Private Life. 50 Cases from Africa for Teaching and Training*, 2019, 235pp. ISBN 978-2-88931-315-0

Readers Series

Christoph Stückelberger, *Global Ethics Applied: vol. 4 Bioethics, Religion, Leadership*, 2016, 426. ISBN 978–2–88931–130–9

Кристоф Штукельбергер, *Сборник статей, Прикладная глобальная этика Экономика. Инновации. Развитие. Мир*, 2017, 224pp. ISBN: 978–5–93618–250–1

CEC Series

Win Burton, *The European Vision and the Churches: The Legacy of Marc Lenders*, Globethics.net, 2015, 251pp. ISBN: 978–2–88931–054–8

Laurens Hogebrink, *Europe's Heart and Soul. Jacques Delors' Appeal to the Churches*, 2015, 91pp. ISBN: 978–2–88931–091–3

Elizabeta Kitanovic and Fr Aimilianos Bogiannou (Eds.), *Advancing Freedom of Religion or Belief for All*, 2016, 191pp. ISBN: 978–2–88931–136–1

Peter Pavlovic (ed.) *Beyond Prosperity? European Economic Governance as a Dialogue between Theology, Economics and Politics*, 2017, 147pp. ISBN 978–2–88931–181–1

Elizabeta Kitanovic / Patrick Roger Schnabel (Editors), *Religious Diversity in Europe and the Rights of Religious Minorities*, 2019, 131pp. ISBN 978-2-88931-270-2

CEC Flash Series

Guy Liagre (ed.), *The New CEC: The Churches' Engagement with a Changing Europe*, 2015, 41pp. ISBN 978–2–88931–072–2

Guy Liagre, *Pensées européennes. De « l'homo nationalis » à une nouvelle citoyenneté*, 2015, 45pp. ISBN : 978–2–88931–073–9

Moral and Ethical Issues in Human Genome Editing. A Statement of the CEC Bioethics Thematic Reference Group, 2019, 85pp. ISBN 978-2-88931-294-8

Philosophy Series

Ignace Haaz, *The Value of Critical Knowledge, Ethics and Education: Philosophical History Bringing Epistemic and Critical Values to Values*, 2019, 234pp. ISBN 978-2-88931-292-4

Ignace Haaz, *Empathy and Indifference: Philosophical Reflections on Schizophrenia*, 2020, 154pp. ISBN 978-2-88931-345-7

Copublications & Other

Patrice Meyer-Bisch, Stefania Gandolfi, Greta Balliu (eds.), *Souveraineté et coopérations : Guide pour fonder toute gouvernance démocratique sur l'interdépendance des droits de l'homme*, 2016, 99pp. ISBN 978–2–88931–119–4

Patrice Meyer-Bisch, Stefania Gandolfi, Greta Balliu (a cura di), *Sovranità e cooperazioni: Guida per fondare ogni governance democratica sull' interdipendenza dei diritti dell'uomo*, 2016, 100pp. ISBN : 978–2–88931–132–3

Patrice Meyer-Bisch, Stefania Gandolfi, Greta Balliu (éds.), *L'interdépendance des droits de l'homme au principe de toute gouvernance démocratique. Commentaire de Souveraineté et coopération*, 2019, 324pp. ISBN 978-2-88931-310-5

Obiora F. Ike, *Applied Ethics to Issues of Development, Culture, Religion and Education*, 2020, 280pp. ISBN 978-2-88931-335-8

Obiora F. Ike, *Moral and Ethical Leadership, Human Rights and Conflict Resolution – African and Global Contexts*, 2020, 191pp. ISBN 978-2-88931-333-4

Reports

Global Ethics Forum 2016 Report, Higher Education—Ethics in Action: The Value of Values across Sectors, 2016, 184pp. ISBN: 978–2–88931–159–0

African Church Assets Programme ACAP: Report on Workshop March 2016, 2016, 75pp. ISBN 978–2–88931–161–3

Globethics Consortium on Ethics in Higher Education Inaugural Meeting 2017 Report, 2018, 170pp. ISBN 978–2–88931–238–2

Managing and Teaching Ethics in Higher Education. Policy, Skills and Resources: Globethics.net International Conference Report 2018, 2019, 206pp. ISBN 978-2-88931-288-7

This is only selection of our latest publications, to view our full collection please visit:

www.globethics.net/publications

www.ingramcontent.com/pod-product-compliance
Lightning Source LLC
LaVergne TN
LVHW050605200726
843508LV00010B/1769